Programming with CodeIgniter MVC

Build feature-rich web applications using
the CodeIgniter MVC framework

Eli Orr

Yehuda Zadik

BIRMINGHAM - MUMBAI

Programming with CodeIgniter MVC

First published: September 2013

Production Reference: 1160913

Published by Packt Publishing Ltd.
Livery Place
35 Livery Street
Birmingham B3 2PB, UK.

ISBN 978-1-84969-470-4

www.packtpub.com

Cover Image by Abhishek Pandey (abhishek.pandey1210@gmail.com)

Credits

Authors
Eli Orr

Yehuda Zadik

Reviewers
Jason Hamilton-Mascioli

Muhammad Faisal Shabbir

Acquisition Editor
James Jones

Commissioning Editor
Shreerang Deshpande

Technical Editors
Dylan Fernandes

Dipika Gaonkar

Kapil Hemnani

Copy Editor
Brandt D'Mello

Aditya Nair

Alfida Paiva

Laxmi Subramanian

Project Coordinator
Deenar Satam

Proofreader
Maria Gould

Indexer
Tejal Soni

Graphics
Ronak Dhruv

Production Coordinator
Melwyn D'sa

Cover Work
Melwyn D'sa

About the Authors

Eli Orr brings over 30 years of experience in the high tech industry, mainly in software product development. Eli published articles in several magazines such as Wireless Systems Design, Telephony-Online, CommsDesign, EE Times, and for various emerging technologies. Currently, Eli is a PHP Advanced Web Application Developer, focused on CodeIgniter based projects for the last two years for rich functionality heavy-duty web applications.

Prior to that, as an entrepreneur, Eli established LogoDial Zappix Ltd., and had the role of CTO and server-side developer. Zappix enables dynamic visualization of call center voice menus, which are currently available in USA and Israel on iOS and Android-enabled smartphones.

Prior to that, Eli developed telecom solutions for Unified Communications with AT&T. Prior to that, Eli developed VoIP developer toolkits as a product manager with Radvision Ltd. During that period, he was an active member with the ITU-T Signaling Group 16 for defining VoIP protocol standardization, mainly the H.323.

Prior to that, Eli led development teams with IAI (Israel Aircraft Industries) ELTA based C and C++ programming languages. Eli can be contacted through his website, http://EliOrr.com.

Wring a book about the CodeIgniter Framework that I use daily and love was a great, thrilling challenge for me.

I would like to thank Yehuda Zadik who assisted me in writing this book as well as the Packt Publishing team for advising and assisting me through the entire book-writing process. In addition, I would like to thank Asher Efrati who is a strong CodeIgniter supporter, who assisted me by reviewing the book drafts and commenting on them. Finally, I would like to thank my daughter Hila Orr who supported me in my effort of writing this book.

Yehuda Zadik has over 20 years of experience in the IT industry, where he mainly specialized in software development based **object-oriented programming (OOP)** technologies.

Yehuda has over 8 years of experience developing with PHP OOP and open source Linux environments for developing web-based applications. Yehuda used state-of-the-art technologies for building dynamic web-based applications that were e-commerce enabled as well as social network integrated. Yehuda has a vast knowledge for integrating third-party plugins for network, mobile, and social environments' integration. Among the environments, Yehuda integrated with Facebook API, LinkedIn API, and various others.

Yehuda is an enthusiastic CodeIgniter developer who has been developing rich functionality and heavy traffic web-based applications over the last two years. Among Yehuda's clients are several major academic institutes. Yehuda can be contacted through his website, `http://yudazdk.co.il`.

Writing this book has been a challenging experience for me. My purpose was to write a practical book for developers that includes many examples.

First of all, I would like to thank my family members, my wife, Elana, and my son, Avishay, for their understanding and support during the writing of this book.

I would like to thank Eli Orr a lot for assisting me in writing the book and his helpful and fruitful feedback.

I would like to thank my clients: Omer Weissbein, CEO of Ontxt, for his advice and support; and Merav Babai, CEO of Pro Man and a LinkedIn expert, for her LinkedIn tips.

Finally, I would like to thank the Packt Publishing team for advising and assisting me throughout the book-writing process.

About the Reviewers

Jason Hamilton-Mascioli leads the growth of `77robots.com`, the Canadian-based web development company he founded in 2005. Jason's role is to find and work with entrepreneurs to produce sustainable online businesses including solutions that aid early-stage startups.

With over 15 years as a senior web developer, Jason has worked with over 100 online startups globally, in addition to providing consulting services and mentorship to early-stage startups and entrepreneurs. For over 6 years, Jason has taught the Building Database-Driven Websites course at McMaster University Continuing Ed based in Hamilton, Ontario, Canada.

Muhammad Faisal Shabbir works as a senior software engineer at Strategic Systems International. Faisal has more than 6 years of extensive experience in software architecture, design, agile development, and deployment. Faisal completed his BS (Information Technology) from Virtual University. He can be reached at `faisal215@gmail.com`.

Special thanks to my mother, wife, and kids, who pushed me up to do such activities.

www.PacktPub.com

Support files, eBooks, discount offers and more

You might want to visit www.PacktPub.com for support files and downloads related to your book.

Did you know that Packt offers eBook versions of every book published, with PDF and ePub files available? You can upgrade to the eBook version at www.PacktPub.com and as a print book customer, you are entitled to a discount on the eBook copy. Get in touch with us at service@packtpub.com for more details.

At www.PacktPub.com, you can also read a collection of free technical articles, sign up for a range of free newsletters and receive exclusive discounts and offers on Packt books and eBooks.

http://PacktLib.PacktPub.com

Do you need instant solutions to your IT questions? PacktLib is Packt's online digital book library. Here, you can access, read and search across Packt's entire library of books.

Why Subscribe?
- Fully searchable across every book published by Packt
- Copy and paste, print and bookmark content
- On demand and accessible via web browser

Free Access for Packt account holders

If you have an account with Packt at www.PacktPub.com, you can use this to access PacktLib today and view nine entirely free books. Simply use your login credentials for immediate access.

Table of Contents

Preface

This book aims to teach you how to develop web applications efficiently with the Ellis Labs CodeIgniter platform. The CodeIgniter platform is an object-oriented Model-View-Controller development platform. For more on MVC, please refer to `http://en.wikipedia.org/wiki/Model-view-controller`. The reader of this book is expected to be familiar with at least the PHP programming language, specifically with PHP OOP (object-oriented programming) and its usage, as well as with MySQL.

CodeIgniter (referred to as CI in this book) is an Application Development Framework, a toolkit for people who build websites and web applications using PHP. CodeIgniter is a smart application development skeleton framework, with flexible and expandable core powered high performance and low footprint. The CodeIgniter framework (OSL 3.0 open source license), developed and maintained by Ellis Labs, powers an echo system of developers across the globe. The first public version of CodeIgniter was released on February 28, 2006. It got very good feedback from web application professional developers. During November 2010, the CodeIgniter development project was added to the well-known GitHub community projects, and got increasing interest and usage by developers worldwide, as well as more and more third parties providing more add-ons with a better maturity and functionality set.

There is a rising trend of web applications based on **OOP (object-oriented programming)** frameworks using **MVC (Model-View-Controller)** development patterns, described in the next section, for developing advanced web applications. CodeIgniter is such a framework. It seems that CodeIgniter is continuously increasing its popularity as it has a simple yet high quality OOP core that enables great creativity, reusability, and code clarity naming conventions, which are easy to expand (user class extends CI class), while more third-party application plugins (including views/controllers/models/libraries/helpers providing application-oriented solutions such as CMS, shopping carts, or table grid navigators) and add-ons of libraries/helpers are becoming available.

The MVC concept is a development pattern or an application framework for a computer user interface that separates the representation of information from the user interacting with it. MVC has been adopted as a successful architecture for web application developments. The model consists of application data and provides services to manipulate them. The controller handles business rules and executes requests to the models and views. The controller mediates between the input, mostly received from a user interacting with a web browser that executed the rendered view. The browser runs a received rendered view by the controller through an HTTP protocol. The controller is the heart of the application. It performs model/database updates, business logic calculations, renders views to the user, and responds to an asynchronous **AJAX (Asynchronous JavaScript and XML)** request sent from the client side. The view code defines the presentation and user input logic to be rendered by the controller as HTML and JavaScript to the browser. The browser receives the rendered view via the HTTP response to be executed locally. The browser executing that content can present data, such as a mix of text, charts, diagrams, and images.

There are legacy **CMS (Content Management System)** web development platforms focused on CMS functionality and maintenance, such as a mature platform named DRUPAL. It might be very useful for content-oriented projects, but less appealing if the project aims to develop a new rich set of functionality, that is, web apps with many inputs and customized UI operations. If the project's requirements involve a low footprint and fast response/high performance, CodeIgniter is found to have excellent results.

To sum up in terms of flexibility, code reusability, light infrastructure, enabling developer creativity, code clarity, highest performance, minimal footprint, and fast learning curve, CodeIgniter seems to be the best choice. Furthermore, it is part of a proactive improvement process thanks to the growing developer's community worldwide.

What this book covers

Chapter 1, Getting Started, introduces the CodeIgniter framework, while initially getting started with web-based applications.

Chapter 2, Configurations and Naming Conventions, reviews the CI naming convention rules, style guide, and spirit as well as the mandatory and optional configurations and usage within a CI project, with several examples. The practice of user-defined configurations will be reviewed as well.

Chapter 3, Controllers, reviews the CI controller and the user-defined controllers extending the CI controller. The CI controller class services, role, definition, usage, and scope will be reviewed with several examples to clarify.

Chapter 4, *Libraries*, reviews the user-defined libraries in a CI framework. Their services, role, definition, usage, and scope will be reviewed with several examples to clarify. Several examples for defining libraries and using them will be provided.

Chapter 5, *Helpers*, introduces you to the CI helpers and user-defined helpers' reusability value, definition rules, scope, and usage. Several examples for defining helpers and using them will be provided.

Chapter 6, *Models*, covers CI models and user-defined models' reusability value, definition rules, scope, and usage. Several examples for defining the models, extending the CI model, and using them will be provided.

Chapter 7, *Views*, explains the CI views concept as the generators for the client-side visualization and user interaction provided via HTTP. The view of the PHP part and scope, visual content (HTML/CSS), and program (JavaScript/AJAX/jQuery) for the client browser will be reviewed. The view's scope, definition, and controller rendering guidelines with practical practice and tips and tricks will be covered in this chapter.

Appendix, *Appendix References*, refers to recommended external resources related to CodeIgniter's formal resources as well as the ECHO system of the developer's community.

What you need for this book
In order to understand this book's content, the user is required to at least have PHP programming language experience with some PHP OOP (object-oriented programming) and MySQL knowledge.

Who this book is for
This book is for PHP web application developers who are interested in developing applications using OOP MVC concepts and specifically the CodeIgniter platform.

Conventions
In this book, you will find a number of styles of text that distinguish between different kinds of information. Here are some examples of these styles, and an explanation of their meaning.

Code words in text are shown as follows: "We can include other contexts through the use of the `include` directive."

A block of code is set as follows:

```
[default]
exten => s,1,Dial(Zap/1|30)
exten => s,2,Voicemail(u100)
exten => s,102,Voicemail(b100)
exten => i,1,Voicemail(s0)
```

When we wish to draw your attention to a particular part of a code block, the relevant lines or items are set in bold:

```
[default]
exten => s,1,Dial(Zap/1|30)
exten => s,2,Voicemail(u100)
exten => s,102,Voicemail(b100)
exten => i,1,Voicemail(s0)
```

Any command-line input or output is written as follows:

```
# cp /usr/src/asterisk-addons/configs/cdr_mysql.conf.sample
    /etc/asterisk/cdr_mysql.conf
```

New terms and important words are shown in bold. Words that you see on the screen, in menus or dialog boxes for example, appear in the text like this: "clicking the **Next** button moves you to the next screen".

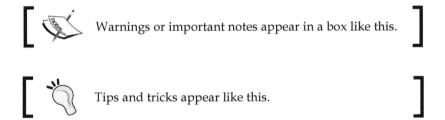

Warnings or important notes appear in a box like this.

Tips and tricks appear like this.

Reader feedback

Feedback from our readers is always welcome. Let us know what you think about this book—what you liked or may have disliked. Reader feedback is important for us to develop titles that you really get the most out of.

To send us general feedback, simply send an e-mail to `feedback@packtpub.com`, and mention the book title through the subject of your message.

If there is a topic that you have expertise in and you are interested in either writing or contributing to a book, see our author guide on www.packtpub.com/authors.

Customer support

Now that you are the proud owner of a Packt book, we have a number of things to help you to get the most from your purchase.

Downloading the example code

You can download the example code files for all Packt books you have purchased from your account at http://www.packtpub.com. If you purchased this book elsewhere, you can visit http://www.packtpub.com/support and register to have the files e-mailed directly to you.

Errata

Although we have taken every care to ensure the accuracy of our content, mistakes do happen. If you find a mistake in one of our books—maybe a mistake in the text or the code—we would be grateful if you would report this to us. By doing so, you can save other readers from frustration and help us improve subsequent versions of this book. If you find any errata, please report them by visiting http://www.packtpub.com/support, selecting your book, clicking on the **errata submission form** link, and entering the details of your errata. Once your errata are verified, your submission will be accepted and the errata will be uploaded to our website, or added to any list of existing errata, under the Errata section of that title.

Piracy

Piracy of copyright material on the Internet is an ongoing problem across all media. At Packt, we take the protection of our copyright and licenses very seriously. If you come across any illegal copies of our works, in any form, on the Internet, please provide us with the location address or website name immediately so that we can pursue a remedy.

Please contact us at copyright@packtpub.com with a link to the suspected pirated material.

We appreciate your help in protecting our authors, and our ability to bring you valuable content.

Questions

You can contact us at questions@packtpub.com if you are having a problem with any aspect of the book, and we will do our best to address it.

1
Getting Started

This chapter covers the basics of the CI development framework and its usage by reviewing some fundamental web application examples. We will start with a basic hello world example and move to an interactive contact-form integration with a database. We will construct the CI applications by following a step-by-step method. Throughout this chapter, we need to remember that the CI development framework is an MVC-based development architecture (for more information, refer to the Wikipedia definition at `http://en.wikipedia.org/wiki/Model-view-controller`).

This chapter will primarily focus on the following topics:

- The CI project directory tree framework
- Configurations (routing and autoloading are covered in this chapter, while the other issues are covered in *Chapter 2, Configurations and Naming Conventions*)
- Example 1: hello world
- Example 2: passing parameters to a view
- Example 3: the database query by a model rendering results to a view
- Example 4: interactive contact forms

By reviewing these examples, we will get the basics of using CI resources. We will begin by briefly reviewing the CI resources used. Then we will review a web application code that loads a static view page. Next we will use the model to retrieve data from a database and show it in a view. Finally, we'll add a view with a contact form to enter input and save it by calling a controller method into the database.

Installing CodeIgniter

First of all, we need to have a hosted PHP server (Version 5.3 or later) and a MySQL (one of the latest versions) server, where we know the database credentials. Local database access from the PHP is recommended for simplicity.

Note that the server will operate in a **CGI** (**Common Gateway Interface**) fashion in order to let CI operate. We can have a local web development environment on our PC or a remote server hosted and dedicated.

Once we've set up a local web development environment, we'll need to download the latest version of CI, which is Version 2.1.2 at the time of writing this book. The link to download the latest version is `http://codeigniter.com/downloads/`. Now, if we look inside the CI folder, we should see the following directory tree:

```
codeigniter/
   index.php
   application/
   cache/
   config/
   controllers/
   core/
   errors/
   helpers/
   hooks/
   language/
   libraries/
   logs/
   models/
   third_party/
   views/
   system/
   core/
   database/
   fonts/
   helpers/
   language/
   libraries/
```

Folders overview

The root folder contains the `index.php` file, which handles all the URI requests. The `index.php` file will process them with the CI core, and apply our application controllers using the models, libraries, and helpers loaded by the controllers and rendered views, `license.txt`, which is the CI's license file. `.htaccess` is used for configuring the CI routing and removing `index.php` from the URL. JavaScript, CSS, and HTML is incorporated into the rendered PHP output and their usage is elaborated in *Chapter 7, Views*.

Let's review the folders and their content application.

The application directory folder is the root directory of our main activity project coding zone. This is the heart of the CI-developed application project.

Mandatory components

Let's take a look at the mandatory components.

- `application/config`: This folder contains all the CI application configuration files, which are covered in *Chapter 2, Configurations and Naming Conventions*.

- `application/controllers`: This folder contains all the application controllers in the CI application project. A controller, as mentioned in the *Preface*, is a component in the MVC-design architecture that handles the request by the user and presents the data shown to the user. A controller in CI is a class extending a base class of the CI controller. The class methods can be executed or called with a proper URI. The naming conventions related to the controller definition and usage will be covered in *Chapter 2, Configurations and Naming Conventions*.

- `application/views`: This folder contains all the view files. A view is the HTML content executed by the user browser that presents and interacts with the user. A view can be a webpage or an RSS page.

The following components are not mandatory but are highly recommended:

- `application/models`: This folder contains all the project model files. A model is the component of the MVC design architecture, which handles the data stored in the database. A model in CI is a PHP class that is designed to work with the information in the database. *Chapter 6, Models*, will elaborate on the CI models concept, definition, and usage with several usage examples.

- `application/helpers`: This folder contains all the additional helper files to the CI helpers. They can be third-party or created by the developer. A helper file is a collection of independent procedural functions in a particular category. Each helper function performs one specific task, with no dependence on other functions. *Chapter 5, Helpers,* will elaborate on the CI helpers concept, definition, and usage with several usage examples.

- `application/libraries`: This folder contains all the libraries of the CI application project created by the developer. A CI library is technically a PHP class. The scope of the library can be any project resource, such as helpers, models, controllers, and views. For example, a library can provide Facebook library API services to simplify the application code for Facebook integration. *Chapter 4, Libraries,* will elaborate on the CI libraries concept, definition, and usage with several usage examples.

- `system`: This is the root of the CodeIgniter core directory. The system folder contains important system components in the subfolders, such as core, database, helpers (built-in system helpers), and libraries (built-in system libraries).

Do not edit any of these files! Upgrading is much easier if we don't.

Example 1 – hello world

Initially, we will start with a simple example that displays **Hello World** on the rendered web page. This is an example that doesn't use a database.

The URI will be `http://ourdomain.com/index.php/hello`.

We can eliminate the `index.php` file from the path to enable a shorter URI; that is, `http://ourdomain.com/index.php/hello`.

In order to enable these shorter URIs, we will make configuration changes as described in *Chapter 2, Configurations and Naming Conventions,* regarding the `config.php` index_page setting in `config.php`.

We will build the following two scripts:

- Controller class: `application/controllers/hello.php`
- View script: `application/views/helloview.php`

In this example, we use the default configuration. For more information about configurations, refer to *Chapter 2, Configurations and Naming Conventions*. The controller in this example passes the parameters that are displayed in the view.

 Passing the parameters from the controller to the view is optional.

The controller file

Here's the code sample of the controller. The controller is responsible for rendering the view with the parameters, such as mega title and message. For naming the controller classes, refer to *Chapter 2, Configurations and Naming Conventions*.

```php
<?php
class Hello extends CI_Controller {
    * Index Page for this controller.
    * Maps to the following URL
        http://example.com/index.php/hello
    - or -
        http://example.com/index.php/hello/index
    - or -
    * since this controller is set as the default controller in
        config/routes.php, it's displayed at http://example.com/
    * So any other public methods not prefixed with an underscore
        will map to /index.php/welcome/<method_name>
    @see http://codeigniter.com/user_guide/general/urls.html
    public function index()
    {
        // Note that $view_params is optional
        // we can use $this->load->view('helloview');as well.
        // if the view doesn't use php variables
        // The $view_params is extracted in the view script to php
        // variables $key = $value
        // In this example three variables will be generated by CI in the
        // view page
        // helloview.php variable: $mega_title
        // value: 'Codeigniter - Hello World'
        // variable: $title      value: 'Welcome to
        // Codegniter'
        // variable: $message     value: 'Hello World'
        $view_params = array(
        'mega_title' => 'Codeigniter - Hello World',
        'title'      =>  'Welcome to Codegniter',
        'message'    =>  'Hello World'
        );
                    $this->load->view('helloview', $view_params);
        }
```

```
} // closing the class definition

/* End of file welcome.php */
/* Location: ./application/controllers/welcome.php */
```

 You can download the example code files for all Packt books you have purchased from your account at http://www.packtpub.com. If you purchased this book elsewhere, you can visit http://www.packtpub.com/support and register to have the files e-mailed directly to you.

The view file

The following is the corresponding rendered view that uses the parameters provided by the controller to render the view to the web page and return it to the user:

```
<!DOCTYPE html>
<html lang="en">
<head>
  <meta charset="utf-8">
  <title><?php echo $mega_title ?></title>
</head>
<body>
  <div id="container">
  <h1><?php echo $title ?></h1>
  <div id="body">
  <p><?php echo $message ?></p>
</div></div>
</body>
</html>
```

Example 2 – passing the complex parameters to a view

In this example, we will show you how to pass and use complex parameters, such as arrays and object arrays, from the CI controller to the rendered CI view to be used in the view. You can pass any number of arrays as parameters to a view; you can also pass objects, such as rows of a query result.

A standard GET parameters URI looks like this: http://ourdomain.com/index.php/example2/more/?a=1&b=2&c=3.

However, let's remember that in CI the URI is passed in this manner: http://ourdomain.com/index.php/example2/more/1/2/3. For more information, see *Chapter 2, Configurations and Naming Conventions*.

Looking at the URI, we will build the controller `example2.php` with the function named `more` with the three parameters passed to it.

We will build the following two scripts:

- The controller class: `application/controllers/example2.php`
- The view script : `application/views/ example2more.php`

The controller file

The controller is responsible for rendering the view with parameters such as mega title and message.

The following is the code sample of the controller:

```php
<?php
class Example2 extends CI_Controller {
  //This function gets parameters and passes them to the view
  //example2more
  //The example url
  //http://ourdomain.com/index.php/example2/more/1/2/3
  so $a = 1, $b = 2, $c = 3
  public function more($a, $b, $c)
  {
    // The parameters in $view_params are extracted in the view
    //example2more.php
    // In this example 2 variables will be generated by CI in the
    //view page example2more.php
    //variable: $mega_title, value: Codeigniter, Passing
    //url parameters to view
    variable: $rows, value: array('a' => $a, 'b' => $b, 'c' => $c);
    $rows = array('a' => $a, 'b' => $b, 'c' => $c);
    $view_params = array('mega_title' => 'Codeigniter -
      Passing url parameters to view 'rows' => $rows);
    $this->load->view('example2more', $view_params);
    }
  }// closing the class definition
/* End of file welcome.php
```

The view file

The following is the corresponding rendered view:

```
<!DOCTYPE html>
<html lang="en">
<head>
  <meta charset="utf-8">
  <title><?php echo $mega_title ?></title>
</head>
<body>
<table>
<tr>
  <td>Key</td>
  <td>Value</td>
</tr>
<?php foreach ($rows as $key => $value): ?>
<tr>
  <td><?php echo $key ; ?></td>
  <td><?php echo $value ; ?></td>
</tr>
<?php endforeach; ?>
</table>
</body>
</html>
```

Example 3 – the database query by a model rendering results to a view

In this example, we will show you how the CI controller uses the CI model to retrieve data from the database and render it to a CI view.

The URL will be `http://ourdomain.com/index.php/user`.

First, we will have to configure the database settings in the configuration file `application/config/database.php`.

We should keep the default database settings unchanged, and only change the following configuration parameters:

```
$db['default']['hostname'] = '127.0.0.1';
//In many cases when the hostname's value is 'localhost' the
connection to the database fails.
//Setting the hostname to 127.0.0.1 solves the problem.
```

```
$db['default']['username'] = 'dbUser;
$db['default']['password'] = 'dbPassword';
$db['default']['database'] = 'dbDataAbse';
$db['default']['port']     = 'dbPort';
```

The model class will retrieve all the user details from the table users.

For more information on configurations, refer to *Chapter 2, Configuration and Naming Conventions*.

We will build the following three scripts:

- The controller class: application/controllers/user.php
- The model file: application/model/usermodel.php
- The view script: application/views/userview.php

The controller file

The controller retrieves the users list from the database via the model and renders the view with it.

The following is the code sample of the controller:

```php
<?php
class User extends CI_Controller {
  function users()
  {
    //Manually loading the database
    $this->load->database();
    //Loading the model class
    $this->load->model('Usermodel');
    $view_params['mega_title'] = 'Model Example';
    //Calling the model to retrieve the users from the database
    $view_params['users']= $this->Usermodel->get_users();
    $this->load->view('userview', $view_params);
  }
}
/* End of file welcome.php */
/* Location: /application/controllers/welcome.php */
```

The model file

The following is the code sample of the model.

```php
<?php
class Usermodel extends CI_Model {
  function __construct()
  {
    // Call the Model constructor    parent::__construct();
  }
  //This method retrieves the users list and returns an array of
  //objects each containing user details
  function get_users()
  {
    //Calling CI's database object's method for generating SQL
    //queries.
    $query = $this->db->get('users');
    //returns an array of users objects
    return $query->result();
  }
}
```

In this example, the CI object database's method is called for generating and executing the SQL query.

Please refer to the CI database's library at `http://ellislab.com/codeigniter/user-guide/database/index.html`.

For more information about models, refer to *Chapter 6, Models*.

The view file

The view in this example shows the table content received from the controller containing the `users` list as defined in the database.

The following is the corresponding rendered view:

```html
<!DOCTYPE html>
<html lang="en">
<head>
  <meta charset="utf-8">
  <title><?php echo $mega_title ?></title>
</head>
<body>
<table>
<tr>
```

```
      <td>ID</td>
      <td>Name</td>
      <td>Email</td>
   </tr>
   <?php foreach ($users as $user): ?>
   <tr>
      <td><?php echo $user->user_id ?></td>
      <td><?php echo $user->user_fname." ".$user->user_lname; ?></td>
      <td><?php echo $user->user_email ; ?></td>
   </tr>
   <?php endforeach; ?>
   </body>
   </html>
```

Example 4 – interactive contact forms

This example shows how to write a contact form using the CI form helper and the `form_validation` library.

For more information about libraries, refer to *Chapter 4*, *Libraries*, and for information about helpers, refer to *Chapter 5*, *Helpers*.

The CI controller defines a form validation setup using the `form_validation` library and renders a form view that uses the `form_validation` library setup to apply a desired validation on the submitted data by the user. If it's a success, the CI controller will render a view page displaying a success message, otherwise it will render the view page with the form and the error messages will be displayed.

The URI for this example is `http://ourdomain.com/index.php/contact`.

In order to perform this example, we shall build the following three scripts:

- The contact form controller class: `application/controllers/contact.php`
- The view form script: `application/views/contactview.php`
- The view success page script: `application/views/contactsuccess.php`

The controller file

The controller creates a form for adding and editing a product.

For more information, refer to *Chapter 7, Views*.

The following is the code sample of the controller:

```php
<?php
class Contact extends CI_Controller {
  public function index()
  {
    //Loading the form helper
    $this->load->helper('form');
    //Loading the form_validation library
    $this->load->library('form_validation');
    $view_params['form']['attributes'] = array('id' =>'myform');
    //contact name details
    $view_params['form']['contact_name']['label'] = array
      ('text' => 'Your name:', 'for' => 'name');
    $view_params['form']['contact_name']['field']= array
      ('name' => 'contact_name', 'id' => 'contact_name',
        'value'=>isset($_POST['contact_name']) ?
    $_POST['contact_name'] : '',
    'maxlength' => '100', 'size' => '30', 'class' => 'input');
    //contact name details
    $view_params['form']['contact_email']['label'] = array
      ('text' => 'Your email:', 'for' => 'email');
    $view_params['form']['contact_email']['field'] = array
      ('name' => 'contact_email', 'id' => 'contact_email',
        'value'=> isset($_POST['contact_email']) ?
    $_POST['contact_email'] : '',
    'maxlength'   => '100', 'size' => '30', 'class' => 'input');
    //contact message details
    $view_params['form']['contact_message']['label'] = array
      ('text' => 'Your message:', 'for' => 'message');
    $view_params['form']['contact_message']['field'] = array
      ('name' => 'contact_message', 'id' => 'contact_message',
        'value' => isset($_POST['contact_message']) ?
    $_POST['contact_message'] : '',
    'rows' => '10',  'cols' => '100', 'class' => 'input');
    // Setting validation rules
    $config_rules = array(array('field' => 'contact_name',
      'label' => 'Contact Name', 'rules' => 'trim|required'),
    array('field' => 'contact_email', 'label' => 'Contact Email',
      'rules' => 'trim|required|valid_email'));
    $this->form_validation->set_rules($config_rules);
    $this->form_validation->set_rules('contact_message',
      'Contact Message', 'trim|required');
    // Validating the form
```

```
    if ($this->form_validation->run() == FALSE)
    // failed
    {
      for ($index = 0; $index < count($a_fields) $index++);
      {
        $s_field = $a_fields[$index];
        if (form_error($s_field))
        {
          $view_params['form'][$s_field]['field']['class'] .= '
            error';
        }
      }
      $this->load->view('contactview', $view_params);
      }
      else // Validation succeeded
      {
      $success_params = array('message'=> 'Success');
      $this->load->view('contactsuccess', $success_params);
      }
    }
  }
}
/* End of file welcome.php */
/* Location: ./application/controllers/welcome.php */
```

The view file

The view file displays the contact form for receiving data from the user.

The following is the corresponding rendered form view:

```
<!DOCTYPE html>
<html lang="en">
<head>
  <meta charset="utf-8">
  <title>Form Example</title>
</head>
<body>
<?php if (validation_errors()) : ?>
  <?php echo validation_errors() ; ?>
  <?php endif; ?>
<?php echo form_open('contact', $form['attributes']) ; ?>
<table>
<tr>
  <td><?php echo form_label($form['contact_name']['label']['text'],
$form['contact_name']['label']['for']);?>
  </td>
  <td><?php echo form_input($form['contact_name']['field']); ?></td>
</tr>
<tr>
```

```
  <td><?php echo form_label($form['contact_email']['label']['text'],
$form['contact_email']['label']['for']);?>
  </td>
  <td><?php echo form_input($form['contact_email']['field']);?>
  </td>
</tr>
<tr>
  <td><?php echo
  form_label($form['contact_message']['label']['text'],
  $form['contact_message']['label']['for']); ?>
  </td>
  <td><?php echo form_textarea($form['contact_message']['field']);?>
  </td>
</tr>
<tr>
  <td colspan="3"><?php echo form_submit('mysubmit', 'Send'); ?></td>
</tr>
</table>
<?php echo form_close() ; ?>
</body>
</html>
The following is the corresponding rendered success view:
<!DOCTYPE html>
<html lang="en">
<head>
  <meta charset="utf-8">
  <title>Contact sent</title>
</head>
<body>
<div id="container">
  <div id="body">
    <p><?php echo $message ?></p>
  </div>
</div>
</body>
</html>
```

Summary

In this chapter we have reviewed the CI directory tree, especially the application folder, which is the heart and soul of any CI project. In the next chapter, we will review the configurations, such as database and naming conventions that are essential for the CI project.

2

Configurations and Naming Conventions

This chapter initially introduces the CI naming conventions. These conventions include the rules, style guide, and CodeIgniter naming spirit. The second part of this chapter will review CI project configurations for built-in resources as well as user-defined or third-party add-on libraries. Note that we will actually build our own project code in the subdirectory application described in *Chapter 1, Getting Started*, with optionally relative resource directories for our project's self-made resources, such as CSS / Media / jQuery libraries' resources or third-party add-ons, extending the base CI downloaded from the Ellis Labs site or GitHub.

We should remember that developing a CI project is done by replacing/expanding the default provided controllers, views, models, and other resources in a well-defined OOP fashion. We should extend controllers, models, and add additional views as well as use defined helpers or libraries. We can add these from third-party libraries or helpers, or develop new ones for our special project business logic and needs.

The initial step after installing the CI is making the proper configurations for our project requirements, such as database, session, auto-loaded helpers, and the libraries we want.

The CI has a set of configuration files defined in the project directory located at `application/config`. These configurations are loaded initially whenever we execute any of our project's CI controllers via a URI call using a browser or issuing an HTTP request via code. The major configuration files are: `config.php`, `database.php`, `autoload.php`, and `routes.php`.

We should review each of the major configuration files with its configuration value, which includes recommended value, and possible values.

CI directory tree

The following is the classic directory tree structure of CodeIgniter:

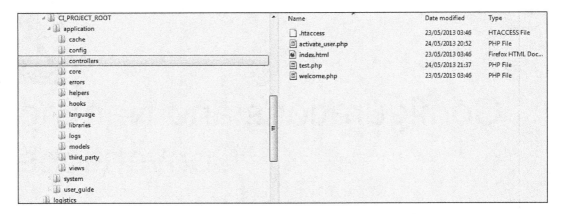

Note that when we add new plugins and other resources such as `bootstrap`, new directories of resources may be added with a name of your choice so that you can refer to them from the specific resource you are developing using the CI `BASEPATH` defined parameter as the directory path to the `CI_PROJECT_ROOT` directory.

If we add a new directory under the project root, let's say `bootstrap`, the path for including resources such as CSS, JavaScript, or images (for example, `hello.png`) will be `$path = BASEPATH."bootstrap/hello.png"`.

config.php

The CI main configuration files have the following major configurations:

```
$config['base_url'] = '';
```

The default is an empty string so that CI can calculate the base URL of our project root directory. We shall refer to the base URL in many places in our code, mostly to execute controllers. To get the base URL, we should call:

```
$base_url = base_url();
// defined in the URL
// helper mentioned before.
```

The `base_url()` function in the URL helper function returns the URI string to the CI project base. For example, if the CI project is developed on a domain named `example.com` under a `public_html` directory named `mydev`, and we have a controller named `find`, a method named `stock`, and a directory named `myprod`, we can call the `find` or `stock` method in both the `myprod` and `mydev` projects using `base_url()`:

```
$url = base_url()."index.php/ find/stock";
```

In the `mydev` project, we will get:

```
$url = "http://example.com/mydev/index.php/find/stock"
```

In the `myprod` project, we will get:

```
$url = "http://example.com/myprod/index.php/find/stock"
```

Hence, in order to call a controller class named `my_class`, we use:

```
$URL = base_url()."index.php/my_class/mymethod";
```

This will define `$url` as `http://example.com/mydev/index.php/my_class`.

To set the index page as a part of the URI path to CI controllers/methods, we use:

```
$config['index_page'] = 'index.php';
```

The `index.php` file is the CI root PHP service that handles all the URI requests. It is used as part of a path URI to a resource, such as `http://mysite.com/fci/index.php/tables_management/show`. However, we can hide the `index.php` file by setting CI to hide the index.php file in the URI path for calling the CI resources such as `http://mysite.com/fci/tables_management/show`. To do so, we need to perform the following configuration steps:

1. In the project root directory where the CI `index.php` file resides, an HTACCESS type file named `.htaccess` is added with the following configuration lines, which reroutes a none `index.php` URI referring to the CI project controllers path without `index.php`:

```
RewriteEngine On
RewriteCond %{REQUEST_FILENAME} !-f
RewriteCond %{REQUEST_FILENAME} !-d

RewriteRule ^(.*)$ index.php/$1 [L]

<Files "index.php">
AcceptPathInfo On
</Files>
```

For more on this, refer to `http://en.wikipedia.org/wiki/Htaccess`.

2. We should make the change to the `/config/config.php` file so that `index_page` will be empty in the URI path string instead of the default `index.php`. `$config['index_page'] = '';`

The `.htaccess` file does the trick here by adding the `index.php` file to the URI after receiving the URI request from the browser and before executing it. The result is that the user who is browsing will not see it, but it will call the desired resource properly, in a similar way to how we used `index.php`:

The language setting is done as follows:

```
$config['language'] = 'english';
```

It is recommended that you leave this as default. Note that even if we use other languages, such as Arabic or Hebrew, it will be fine. We just make sure that our PHP files are saved as UTF-8 without BOM (byte order mark is a unicode character that marks the file-encoding method supporting multilanguage schemes; for more information, refer to `http://en.wikipedia.org/wiki/Byte_order_mark` to inform the browser that receives the rendered HTML page to process it as a UTF-8 file.

The exact meaning of this tag is out of the scope of this book and can be learned from HTML standard.

```
$config['charset'] = 'UTF-8';
```

Additionally, it is highly recommended for multi-language support to add the following line in our view file's HTML header:

```
<meta http-equiv="Content-Type"
content="text/html; charset=utf-8" />
```

These settings inform the browser to process the rendered HTML page whose characters are encoded as UTF-8, which is the most common multilanguage standard for non-English languages such as Hebrew, Arabic, and Chinese.

Do not touch these settings; it is very useful to support multiple languages.

```
$config['enable_hooks'] = FALSE;
```

The preceding configuration, if set to TRUE, will enable us to define hooks into CI events, where the hooks are defined in the `application/hooks` directory. Do not touch these settings unless you have a specific plan for CI event hooks. Note that the concept of adding hooks to the CI core activity is out of this book's scope.

```
$config['subclass_prefix'] = 'MY_';
```

The preceding configuration will enable us to define naming roles to our library class name's prefix, in order to distinguish with other default libraries.

```
$config['permitted_uri_chars'] = 'a-z 0-9~%.:_\-';
```

The preceding code defines the allowed chars within a URI calling CI resources, mainly controllers. It is recommended to not touch this setting.

```
$config['allow_get_array'] = TRUE;
```

This will enable us to call the controller class methods with parameters, such as in the example provided earlier.

```
<?php echo base_url(); ?>index.php/my_handler/calc/5/7
```

The preceding code will provide the same results as the class method within the my_handler class itself in the following format:

```
$Val= $this->calc(5,7);
```

The following configuration defines if a GET URL query string will be used:

```
$config['enable_query_strings'] = FALSE;
```

This configuration, if set to TRUE, will enable us to call controller class methods with parameters in the GET URL query form:

```
<?php echo base_url();?>index.php/my_handler/calc.php?a=5&b=7
```

It is highly recommended to leave this as FALSE, as CI provides a solution to pass parameters within URI, as shown in the calc example at the beginning of this chapter.

The log threshold for the severity level is such that any event that is of the same or higher severity level will be logged to CI. The supported threshold levels and their meanings are as follows:

- **0**: Disables logging (error logging turned off)
- **1**: Error messages (including PHP errors)
- **2**: Debug messages
- **3**: Informational messages
- **4**: All messages

```
$config['log_threshold'] = 4;
// 4 is the highest level for all CI events from notice level
// events and worse
```

The preceding configuration will generate error logs according to the `log_threshold ()` level at `/application/logs` if the error log was enabled.

Note that enabling the errors log will cause performance reduction in our web application. Use it only if you must for debugging needs. Otherwise set it to `0`.

```
$config['log_path'] = '';
```

The default log file path in the CI project is `application/logs`. Do not touch this configuration unless you have a clear reason.

The date time format:

```
$config['log_date_format'] = 'Y-m-d H:i:s';
```

The default date time format setting is `2012-06-18 14:54:11`. It is recommended to not touch this configuration.

The cache file path:

```
$config['cache_path'] = '';
```

The default is `application/cache`. It is recommended not to touch this configuration. The session key:

```
$config['encryption_key'] = '';
```

This `encryption_key` must be set with a key in order to use the session class services. For example:

```
$config['encryption_key'] =
'cMGy4DSwGUvxYSar4279626HgOn2342efrwerr2TE2RF4G3reg4tF3etf';
```

An example of the session library usage within a controller and setting a session variable is as follows:

```
$uid = 119; // where uid is the id of the loggeing user
$this->session->set_userdata ('this_user_id', $uid );
```

Getting the session variable in another controller is as follows:

```
$uid = $this->session->userdata('this_user_id');
```

The session data storage mechanism is as follows:

```
$config['sess_use_database'] = FALSE;
```

If the recommended configuration is set to `TRUE`, we would use many session parameters of a large size stored in the associated default database.

Session expiration timeout in seconds:

```
$config['sess_expiration'] = 7200;
// The number of seconds the session will be kept
```

Additional session configuration parameters can be found in the CI user manual. Cross-site scripting (XSS) filtering activation/deactivation:

```
$config['global_xss_filtering'] = FALSE;
```

This will enable XSS filtering on URI requests sent to the application. Note that all URI requests are processed initially by the root index.php to analyze the URI request and issue the proper CI calls. If set to TRUE it will protect URI requests from XSS type malicious attackers. It is recommended to set it to TRUE even if we reduce a bit of our application performance.

```
$config['csrf_protection'] = FALSE;
```

If set to TRUE the CI will prevent **Cross-Site Request Forgery (CSRF/XSRF)** attacks. The risk is when the fraud form is submitted. If we are accepting user data, it is strongly recommended that CSRF protection should be enabled. Note that when using AJAX, additional code may be required to enable CSRF protection with AJAX.

database.php

The database configuration enables to define one or more database connections that can be used by the application. The database configuration is a two-dimensional array in the following form:

```
$db['db_entry']['db_connection_param']
```

By setting the parameters for database default entry, we shall define the following parameters:

```
$db['default']['hostname'] = 'localhost';
// note: in some cases '127.0.0.1' must be used instead
// localhost if the database server is in another server use
// URI such as: 'domain.db.NNNNNNN.hostedresource.com' or
// similar - advise our system admin/service provider
// Optional configuration of DB server connection port

$db['default']['port'] = '4009';
// In case our DB server operates on another port
// otherwise we may drop the port config line!

$db['default']['username'] = 'mydefaultdb';
```

```
$db['default']['password']  =  'mypass1';
$db['default']['database']  =  'mydatabase1';
$db['default']['dbdriver']  =  "mysql";
$db['default']['dbprefix']  =  "";
$db['default']['pconnect']  =  TRUE;
$db['default']['db_debug']  =  TRUE;
$db['default']['cache_on']  =  TRUE;
$db['default']['cachedir']  =  "";
$db['default']['char_set']  =  "utf8";
$db['default']['dbcollat']  =  "utf8_general_ci";
```

By setting the parameters for another database entry named dbentry2, we shall define the following parameters:

```
$db['dbentry2']['hostname']  =  'localhost';
$db['dbentry2']['username']  =  'mySecondDB';
$db['dbentry2']['password']  =  'mypass2';
$db['dbentry2']['database']  =  'mySecondDB';
$db['dbentry2']['dbdriver']  =  "mysql";
$db['dbentry2']['dbprefix']  =  "";
$db['dbentry2']['pconnect']  =  TRUE;
$db['dbentry2']['db_debug']  =  TRUE;
$db['dbentry2']['cache_on']  =  TRUE;
$db['dbentry2']['cachedir']  =  "";
$db['dbentry2']['char_set']  =  "utf8";
$db['dbentry2']['dbcollat']  =  "utf8_general_ci";
```

There is no need to connect and load the default database as it is done automatically when loading the database class — however, the call is:

```
$this->load->database();
```

Or, for referring to a specific database entry name, it is:

```
$this->load->database('default');
```

In order to connect and load the dbentry2 database settings stated earlier, use the following code:

```
$this->dbentry2= $this->load->database(dbentry2', TRUE);
```

To use the default database with the database class library, db, use:

```
$q1 = $this->db->query ("select * from mytable");
```

To use the dbentry2 database, use:

```
$q2 = $this->dbentry2->db->query ("select * from DB2table");
```

routes.php

Define the default controller that will be executed when referred via the URI to the base_url of the project—let's say http://mydomain.com/myapp so that myapp is a subdirectory of public_html in the sever and we have home_page_controller.

```
$route['default_controller'] = "home_page_controller";
```

When the user issues http://mydomain.com/myapp, due to the route configuration for the home controller, the URI that CI will issue will be as if the user is referring to http://mydomain.com/myapp/home_page_controller.

```
$route['404_override'] = '';
```

In the preceding example, the default application/errors/error_404.php page will be executed, in case the user refers to a non-existing project controller, such as http://mydomain.com/myapp/sadfasdfsdfsdi.

We may decide, for example, to pop-up a message for the non-existing page and route to the default URI to minimize user inconvenience.

Defining and using your own configurations

CI enables us to define our own configurations and easily access them via the config class. For example, with application/config/my_config.php, let's say we define a parameter in that config file as follows:

```
$param1 = "value1";
```

We can easily access our configuration file parameters to load all the parameters into the array:

```
$array = $this->config->load('my_config', TRUE);
```

The second parameter, TRUE, assures us that our configuration parameters will be defined in an array prefixed with the configuration file name.

Consider: $param1 = $array['my_config']['param1'];

or: $param1 = $this->config->item('param1', 'my_config');.

$param1 will have the value value1 that we have set in the configuration file that we built.

Understanding and using CI naming conventions

The CI naming conventions are essential to understand and use, in order to properly develop with CI. They enable you to write minimal code using a strict and concise set of rules.

The full CI naming conventions and style guide can be found at `http://codeigniter.com/user_guide/general/styleguide.html`.

The naming conventions refer to the naming of parameters, functions/methods, class-related PHP file name storing code, project resource paths, and so on. Here are the specific issues we will review:

- Extending CI resources such as the CI controller or model in our project resources (class extends class fashion—for example, extending `CI_controller` or `CI_model`; see the examples discussed in the *Controller definition naming rules* section)

- Defining views and rendering them by a controller with or without providing parameters that the view code may use for its operation

- Using existing general reusable resources (can be loaded from any controller or model and reused by rendered views as well) of CI helpers and libraries, and defining new CI helpers and libraries

- How-tos, dos, and don'ts for locating files and naming are categorized based on the defined controllers, models, libraries, and helpers

- Relations between the defined class resource name, containing file name, loading a defined class a helper or a model, instantiating and calling a calls method via the URI and calling a class method with parameters

The main resource type naming rules

CI defines "one class one file standard" so that every class of a CI controller extension and CI model extension of a library class resides in one file. This also applies to helpers that are a set of functions. Each resource category (controller, library, model, and view) will be located in a specific directory or its subdirectory. The most commonly used resource categories are as follows:

- **Controllers**: These get the client side (for example, browser) to operate

- **Views**: These are rendered by the controller and returned to the browser via HTTP

- **Libraries**: These are called by project resources such as controllers, views, models, and helpers

- **Models**: These are called by project resources such as controllers, views, libraries, and helpers

- **Helpers**: These are called by project resources such as controllers, views, libraries, and models

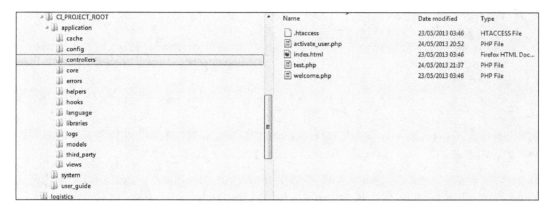

Controller definition naming rules

Let's define the initial project controller to handle some basic services. Note that the controller class name is `My_handler`, and must reside in a file named `my_handler.php` (all lower case) at `/application/controllers` in our CI project directory. Here's the code sample with which to review the naming conventions:

```
class My_handler extends CI_Controller {
function __construct(){
// Must Call Patent to get all its services inherited
parent::__construct();
}
   function index () {
// executed when referring to My_handlercontroller via URLecho "Hello
World"; }

function calc  ($a = 2, $b=2) {
// executed when referring to My_handler/calc via URL echo    " $a * $b
= ".$a*$b;
}


functionAJAX_calc () {
// If the request is not an AJAX we shall abort!
//This is done by the
```

```
if (!$this->input->is_AJAX_request())
exit ('none AJAX calls rejected!');
// see http://codeigniter.com/user_guide/libraries/input.html

$a = $this->input->post('a');// get the posted a parameter
$b = $this->input->post('b');// get the posted b parameter

$result = (int) $a * (int) $b;
$data = array('result'=> $result);
// to add more array parameters: ,'p2' => $p2, 'p3'=>$p3,..
echojson_encode($data);// return the JSON encoded array
return;
}

} // closing the class definition
```

We call this controller via an HTTP request URL, as an HTTP or HTTPS request. For example: `http://mydomain.com/index.php/my_handler`.

Let us review several usage scenarios with this controller class definition. Note that you can enable CodeIgniter to operate without the `index.php` file in the path; for more information, refer to the `index.php` file issue discussed later in this chapter. In this section we will review different use cases for the CI controller as well as the naming rules associated with the controller. The following are the cases that are mainly used for calling a controller:

- Directly from a browser
- From a view HTML page script using a CI PHP anchor helper embedded in the page
- From a view HTML page using a JavaScript/jQuery AJAX call embedded in the page
- From a crontab PHP script using cURL to call a controller

The controller has its own naming rules and usage guidelines that we will review now. The controller is most commonly called from the view using an anchor tag. However, it may also be called using AJAX or even a crontab PHP script using a PHP function file or cURL-based request.

Example 1 – calling the controller index method

Controllers are mostly called via a user interaction session on a rendered view processed by a client browser. The controller method is called to issue another process, such as and AJAX request or processing the request and rendering it back to the client browser additional view or web page. To define the controller call within a view definition (application/views), we define an anchor to be executed by the browser per user request. Note that in these examples we use another URL helper named `anchor()`.

```
anchor( $uri, $text, $html_attributes);
```

Note that in order to use the CI anchor helper function, we will initially load the helper URL via `config/autoload.php`.

```
$autoload['helper'] = array('url');
```

Another way to do this is to load the anchor helper in the controller rendering the view, where we want to use an anchor:

```
$this->load->helper('url');
```

- `$URI`: The URI path to call a controller or any URI we want to execute
- `$text`: The anchor label shown to the user to click on
- `$html_attributes`: Any HTML attributes that can be defined for an HTML anchor element

An example of the resulting HTML that will be executed by the client-side browser is as follows:

```
<a href="myapps.com/myciapp/showme" class='mybutton'>
Press Me
</a>
<!-- where        $uri = 'myapps.com/myciapp/showme';
$text = 'Press Me';
$html_attributes = "class='mybutton'";-->
```

Back to our example—the view code part that enables the user to call the defined controller will look like the following (the PHP portions are with other HTML tags in a view file):

```
<?PHP
echo anchor(ase_url().' index.php/my_handler ','Press Me A');
?>
```

Since we only referred to the class name, its constructor and index method, if defined, will be executed. In case we did not define an index method for this `my_handler` controller, the preceding calls will only instantiate the class using its constructor definition, and if the index method was defined it will be called as well. In our case, the index method was defined so it will be called as well.

Example 2 – calling the controller and calc method without arguments

In this example, we enable the end user to call a specific class method but without parameters, so that the default method parameters must be used via the browser.

Note that in order to use any CI helper function we need to make sure that it is either autoloaded or specifically loaded in the controller (for the controller method's usage or rendered views), library, or model.

```
<?PHP
echo anchor(base_url().' index.php/my_handler/calc ' ,'Press Me B');
?>
```

Note that in order to refer to a specific `My_handler` class method named `calc`, we concatenated `/calc` after the class name. Issuing this view from a browser we will get a result as follows: **2 * 2 = 4. Why?**.

This is simply because we define default values in the receiving controller method. So that if no parameters are sent as in this example the default ones will be used, which are both set to 2 and hence the class `calc` method will output 4.

Example 3 – calling the controller and calc method with arguments

In this example we enable the end user to call a specific class method with its parameters via the browser.

```
<?PHP
echo anchor(base_url().' index.php/my_handler/calc/5/7', 'Press Me
C',);
?>
```

Issuing this from a browser, we will get: **5 * 7 = 35. Why?**.

Since we provided 5 as the first parameter and 7 as the second, using the CI URI naming convention of spectated / to pass parameter values to a called controller class method. Since we use the parameters as integers for multiplication, PHP casts them as integers, so we have 5 * 7 which is 35.

Note that in order to call a specific controller method with parameters, we add the / separator after the method name followed by the parameters, and each parameter is also separated by /.

To understand this better see the following use cases and their meanings, CI uses the URI as follows:

When issuing the URI:

```
<?PHP base_url() ?>/controller_name/method_name/param1/param2/../
paramN
```

The controller named `controller_name` will be instanced by CI with the controller constructor, and then the method `method_name` will be called with the first parameter `param1`, second parameter `param2`, and so on.

On the PHP controller side, the `controller_name` method prototype will look like the following example:

```
Publicfunction method_name($user, $name, $email, $phone) {
```

So that `$user` = param1, `$name` = param2, and so on.

This is one possible way to get the parameters through a URL or get an array. In CodeIgniter we don't have to get an array, so we can use the URI class to get the parameters. For reference, see `http://ellislab.com/codeigniter/user-guide/libraries/uri.html`.

If we provide:

```
<?PHP base_url() ?>/controller_name
```

The CI will execute only the controller constructor and the `index()` method, if the controller has such a method.

If we provide:

```
<?PHP base_url() ?>/controller_name/method_name
```

The preceding code will be executed without calling the index() method, following the call of the specific method, method_name. Remember that we shall not use / in our parameters for such a call and may wish to provide them using URL encode or other reversible encoding methods. We can also call our controller method using POST/GET so that we can retrieve the parameter value posted in the class method in the following way:

```
$param1_val = $this->input->post('param1');
```

For example, within the class code we issue an AJAX call to a function as shown in the next example.

Example 4 – calling AJAX to an AJAX-oriented method with arguments

In this example we enable the end user to issue an AJAX call to a specific class method with its parameters enabled via HTTP POST.

```
<script src="https://AJAX.googleapis.com/AJAX/libs/jquery/1.8.1/
jquery.min.js">
</script>
<script type="text/javascript">

function AJAX_call () {

a_val  = $('[name="a"]').val();
b_val  = $('[name="b"]').val();
AJAX_url =
'<?PHP echo base_url()."index.php/my_handler/AJAX_calc";?>';
$.AJAX({
type: "POST",
url : AJAX_url,
data: {a : a_val,  b : b_val },
dataType: "json",
success: function(data)
{$('#result').html (data.result); }
}); // AJAX Call end
}</script>

<form onsubmit="AJAX_call();">
  <label>Enter A</label><input type="text" name="a" />
  <label>Enter B</label><input type="text" name="b" />
  Result:<div id='result'>The Result Will Be Shown Here</div>
  <input type="submit" value="Calculate" />
</form>
```

Enter two numeric values for A and B and click on the **Calculate** button. We will get the integer casted as A and multiply it by the integer casted as B in the div section with id='result'.

Loading libraries, models, and helpers

To reuse other libraries, models, and helper capabilities in our controller, we may also want to load libraries and helpers to our controller or model class to reuse them for our needs. In case we decide that certain helpers, libraries, or models are useful, we will have them loaded automatically. We can do so in the autoload configuration file named autoload.php located at application/config/autoload.php in our project.

The following is an autoload configuration example:

```
$autoload['libraries'] = array('template','database','session');

$autoload['helper'] =
array('url', 'utilities');

// Note: url helper provide base_url() service
```

Remember that if we want to load our helpers or libraries within a certain controller or model, we can enable it as per the following example:

```
classMy_handler extends CI_Controller {
function __construct(){
// see previous explanation on this parent call
parent::__construct();

// Loadingspecific helperto enable calling
// its functions in all this
// controller class methods as well as in all
// rendered views.
// Note how the full name and path is abbreviated:

$this->load->helper('ssl_helper');

//Loading and instantiatinga library s
// application/librarues/smart_handler.php to
// enable calling all its class methods as from
// this controller as well from all the rendered
// by this controller.
$this->load->library('smart_handler' );
}
function enforce_ssl () {
```

```
force_ssl();
// A function in the ssl_helper for more see
// helpers chapter
}
function smarty () {
//call a method smart_service in the loaded //smart_handler library
//for more see Libraries chapter
$this->smart_handler->smart_service($param1, $param2);
}
}//End Controller My_handler
```

We shall call the method that uses the helper as follows:

```
<?php echo base_url(); ?>index.php/my_handler/enforce_ssl
```

For smarty method calls in the loaded library, we use the following code:

```
<?php echo base_url(); ?>index.php/my_handler/smarty
```

Passing parameters within a controller into a view, `application/controllers/my_controller.php` as follows:

```
$array = array ('a' =>100,'b' =>200);
$view_params = array
('param1' => 'hello world',
'param2' =>$array
);
$this->load_view('my_view', $view_params);
```

In the view file at `application/views: my_view.php`, the view can use the provided parameters in the following method:

```
<?PHP
echo $param1;// will echo hello world
```

Note that within the controller it is defined as the `param1` key array element, where the array is sent to the view.

```
// To get the param2 values we shall perform :

foreach ( $params2 as param ){
echo param;
// will echo 100 and 200 as $params2['a'] and
// $params2['b'] values
}
?>
```

Miscellaneous naming conventions

CI guidelines have some general naming conventions, such as the following:

- Your classes, functions, and parameters should have short names, and if constructed from several words they should use the underscore separator as follows:

```
// several lowercase words naming with under score
get_file_properties();
```

- When defining a string value, in case the string does not have a parameter to evaluate, we shall use a single comma as follows:

```
$my_string    = 'the string';
```

- In case we want our string to have a parameter such as $name, we write our string using double quotes:

```
$name = 'big string parameter';
$my_string = "This is a $name ";
```

- The Boolean and contacts all should be in upper case:

```
$this_vale = FALSE;
// While in javascript we shall use true / false
// to distinguish
```

For more general CI PHP style guide refer to http://codeigniter.com/user_guide/general/styleguide.html.

Summary

In this chapter we have reviewed and practiced CI naming conventions, rules, and usage with a set of examples for parameters, classes, controllers, models, helpers, libraries, and views.

Following the naming conventions we have reviewed CI configurations. We reviewed the major configuration files, such as config.php, database.php, autoload.php, and routes.php in depth. We also reviewed how we can use the configuration parameters while configuring several databases to be used in our project. In addition to it we also saw how we can add more project-specific configurations.

3
Controller Usage and Scope

This chapter covers the CI controller scope and the various controller usage categories with several code examples of web applications. The controllers are the front-line decision makers of how to process or route a request and how to respond to actions, such as a rendered view sending back to the browser as an HTML page, an AJAX response to let the current requesting page update certain selector areas by the response, or even just to update the database seamlessly. The controllers use the available models, helpers, libraries, and views to respond to the caller, be it a web browser URL or a cron process issuing the cURL types POST/GET requests automatically.

The CI built-in controller behaves like an abstract class in the project scope so any of our project controllers must be extensions of a built-in CI controller. Our developed controller will inherit the CI built-in controller capabilities and built-in resources, such as auto-loaded helpers, libraries, and models, and let us code any specific services as controller methods to address our project requirements, and rendering the needs of the view.

As mentioned before, the controller is part of the MVC development framework that operates with models, and applies business logic, which most commonly renders a view back to the client web browser to proceed with user interaction.

The web user refers, via a browser, to a URL. In CI, the view is implemented as a call to a CI controller method. The CI controller method processes the browser request and sends back a rendered view that becomes a visualized web page to the browsing user.

The web page received from the CI controller is referred to as the rendered controller view; it may include anchors and buttons for the user to continue the interaction with the controller. When the user clicks on an anchor in the browser, a call to a controller is made (the anchor makes an HTTP request to activate a controller call). In case the user issue a event such as Button clicking, operate scroll bars, and so on so that this user event will trigger an action using jQuery to activate, for example a jQuery callback function. The jQuery callback function may issue a call to another rendering controller, such as :

```
$(location).attr('href',controller_url_to_call);
```

Another option is to activate an asynchronous AJAX calls to an AJAX controller. Such a controller function handles the AJAX request that we will discuss later on. When AJAX calls returned from the server , their returned data may be used by client-side JavaScript to, update certain page regions/ (HTML selector/s) of the web page, for example, when typing a search string and issuing a search button, the AJAX response will provide the search results to be visualized in the same web page or will move to another page.

More on controllers in general can be found at http://en.wikipedia.org/wiki/Model-view-controller.

The following are the chapter topics and subtopics we will cover:

- Scope of the CI controller
- Usage categories:
    - Rendering views
    - Controllers serving browser AJAX requests
    - Controllers serving Linux scheduled cron execution requests
- CI controller expansion and usage( )(Refer to *Chapter 2, Configurations and Naming Conventions*, for more)
    - Loading resources of models, helpers, and libraries
    - Using loaded resources
    - Calling CI controller methods
- Example 1: the default home page controller
- Example 2: sending e-mails with attachments
- Example 3: admin and regular user log in

We will begin by briefly reviewing the scope and use cases of the application controller in the CI framework and how we can use them for our project requirement needs.

Scope of the CI controller

The CI controller is the hub and brain of the CI MVC that handles the HTTP requests, such as those from the browser, and operates with other CI resources to respond. The CI controller scope is described in the following figure and operates with other CI resources to respond to the requests:

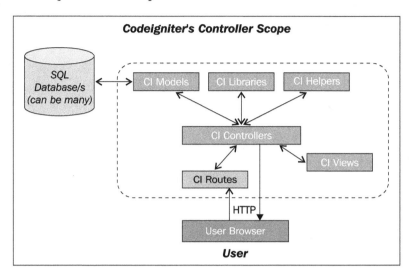

The general flow with the CI controller is shown in the preceding figure. The user's browser sends the HTTP request to the URL of the CI project. Initially, the requested URL is processed via the routes based on the routes configuration /conf/routes.php. For more information, refer to *Chapter 2, Configurations and Naming Conventions*. The specific CI controller is instantiated and the specific method is called. The CI method may be assisted by any of the project resources, such as models, libraries, and helpers for operations (business logic, and database queries). The CI controller generally uses a view that defines a web page to be responded to via an HTTP response.

The user-defined CI controller

Each CI project must have one or more user-defined controllers in order to operate. The user-defined controllers are the starting point of any CI user interaction. Calling the controller and its methods can be done in several ways. The controller can be called via project root URI submission to a browser (the project default controller will be called), by issuing the user anchor from a rendered view, by a client-side AJAX request for actions (updating page selectors), or even by a `crontab` (Linux known scheduler service) scheduled action executed repeatedly as a URI of a certain controller method.

We can see that the controller scope is a general manager of all the other project resources, such as models, views, helpers, and libraries, governing all to address execution requests from the user or a scheduled request.

Any application controller will be located under `application/controller/` in the `project` directory.

The controller can load other CI project code resources of libraries, models, and helpers so that they can be accessed directly by the rendered views. This means that, if a controller loaded a library, the rendered view PHP file can call the library function in the exact same way as the controller does. The following is the code resources that the controller can load:

- `application/helpers`: The helper/s are built-in CI third-party, or user-defined.

- `application/models`: The models are most commonly user-defined for the specific database/s and tables of the specific project, extending the built-in CI model. Wrapping with CRUD service for specific defined database/s table/s, but also can be third-party (for example, data mapper extensions that can be used generically with any database).

- `application/libraries`: The library can be built-in, third-party, or user-defined. The library is an Object Oriented PHP class-based service that can provide some reusable services related to a specific project, or across many projects. For example, as Flickr, Facebook, or LinkedIn wrapper API libraries. A good practice is to define in addition to the third-party libraries we may decide to use, our project oriented libraries to enhance our project simplicity, and maintainability.

Extending the CI controller

As we said, our application controller extends the built-in CI controller that is something like an abstract class in the development scope, so that in order to use the controller for our needs, we must build our controller extending the base class. We can extend the CI controller in several ways.

- Loading resources of helpers, models, and libraries:
  - ° Those can be from the CI built-in repository, third-party developed, or self-developed. For more information on how to self-develop models, refer to *Chapter 6, Models*, on how to self-develop libraries, refer to *Chapter 4, Libraries*, and on how to self-develop helpers, refer to *Chapter 5, Helpers*.
  - ° The controller can load any of the external resources in the following fashion in any of its methods, commonly at the contractor and in case the resource is required in all the controllers via the `autoload.php` configuration file ( ) (refer to *Chapter 3, Configurations and Naming Conventions* for more information). However, for the best resource optimization to minimize the footprint and overhead even better, the resources will be loaded only on those controller methods that need their services to operate.

  The following are a few examples of how to load the mentioned resources:

  ```
  $this->load->model('some_model');
  $this->load->library('some_library', $keyed_array);
  $this->load->helper('some_helper');
  ```

- Adding public and private methods:
  - ° This approach is the common guideline of PHP OOP that you are expected to be familiar with (although elaboration on this can be found at `http://php.net`). The following is a simple example of how a public method calls a private method to get some data:

    ```
    public function get_something () {
      $some_data= $this->_get_it ();
      }
    private function _get_it () {
      return= 'hello';
      }
    ```

- Using loaded resources:

  The loaded resources can be used after loading as follows:

  ° Using loaded model methods:

    ```
    $status= $this->some_model->save_data($table, $row);
    $rows= $this->some_model->get_table($table_name);
    ```

  ° Using loaded library methods:

    ```
    $another_data = $this->some_library->method($some_data);
    ```

  ° Using loaded helpers:

    ```
    $your_ip =get_your_ip();   // myhtml_helper function
    // NOTE: a helper defines regular functions!
    ```

- Calling a controller:

  ° The controller is automatically instantiated by the CI core, and its methods are called via HTTP URIs. For more information, refer to *Chapter 2, Configurations and Naming Conventions.*

  ° Ways to call a controller:

    Calling only the contractor and later calling the index method, if defined as follows: `$URI = "base_url().'/mycontroller';` mycontroller';

    Calling the method of the `mycontroller` class without parameters: `$URI = "base_url.'/mycontroller/mymethod';`

    Calling the method of the `mycontroller` class with two parameters, a and b: `$URI = "base_url.'/mycontroller/mymethod/a/b';`

CI controller use cases

There are several different use cases for a CI user-defined controller. Commonly, the CI controller will handle initiating/rendering HTML pages, enable us to let the user navigate and view the different web application pages we defined. However, the controller may also provide other services, such as AJAX server-side controller, serving asynchronously the client-side browser requests, and commonly return back the JSON formatted data instead of a rendered view. The exact scope and usage of AJAX is not part of the CI framework, but it is very useful standard de-facto technology. To learn more about AJAX, please refer to AJAX (Asynchronous JavaScript and XML) on Wikipedia `http://en.wikipedia.org`.

The main usage categories for our controller in a CI framework are as follows:

- Rendering views: These type of controllers mostly performs some preparations for data and render the requested view, along with the prepared data, to be displayed to the user for the next user session state with web application.

- A special case is the home page view rendering. So that the user refers to the Project root directory via URI such as:

  `http://mydomain.com/my_ci_project`.

- Where the CI routes will define `maincontroller` as the home page or default controller as follows under the project root:`application/config/routes.php`. So that the default controller will be defined as follows:

  `$route ['default_controller'] = "maincontroller";`

- Then the call to

  `http://mydomain.com/my_ci_project will be routed by the CI routes`

  to

  `http://mydomain.com/my_ci_project/maincontroller`

  For user navigation request to another page, we shall have in the rendered view, HTML anchors for navigating into another pages something like the following view code:

```php
<?PHP echo anchor
   (site_url().'/pages_controller/page_b',
     'Navigate me to page B'); ?>
```

- Controller serving the browser AJAX requests. These controllers respond to the AJAX client requests. and most commonly return the JSON data to the calling jQuery script as follows:

```
<script type="text/javascript">
function autocomplete(clue_val) {
  varurl = '<?php echo site_url();
    ?>/AJAX_controller/autocomplete_name';
  $AJAX ({type: "POST", url: url, data: {clue: clue_val},
    dataType: "json", success: function(data) {
      // show the data of matching names
      }
    return;
    });
```

- Controller serving Linux scheduled `cron` requests: A very powerful CI usage we found is serving Linux `cron` schedule requests defined in the Linux `cron` (for more information about Linux `cron` scheduling, please refer to `http://en.wikipedia.org/wiki/Cron`).

We can find, within the **DirectAdmin** apache admin tool, a UI editor to define the scheduled `crontab` repeatable actions we want the server to perform.

For each request, we will define the PHP processor path; for example, `/user/local/bin/php`, as well as the PHP script to be executed; for example, `/home/mysite.com/public_html/crontabs/ci_crontab.php`.

`ci_crontab.php` can execute the CI controller method.

`http://myCIproject/mycontroller/mymethod` will, for example, scan the database and update a table named `sums_table`, which contains the number of rows in all the tables added together after every execution. Let us see an example of how to make that CI controller call from the PHP script.

In order to call a CI controller via an HTTP request, `ci_crontab.php` will use the cURL service that will call the CI controller, similar to the way we issue it from a browser (**cURL (Client URLs)**, `http://php.net/manual/en/ref.curl.php`).

Let's build `/home/mysite.com/public_html/crontabs/ci_crontab.php`.

Linux crontab will call every defined action repeatedly.

The code of `ci_crontab.php` will be something like the following code:

```
<?PHP
function file_get_contents_curl($url) {
  $ch = curl_init();
  curl_setopt($ch, CURLOPT_HEADER, 0);
  curl_setopt($ch, CURLOPT_RETURNTRANSFER, 1);
  curl_setopt($ch, CURLOPT_URL, $url);
  $data = curl_exec($ch);
  curl_close($ch);
  return $data;
  }
$http_to_execut='http://myCIproject/mycontroller/mymethod';
$result = file_get_contents_curl ($http_to_execute);
```

The `$result` will be the rendered output from the controller, mostly simple echoed messages such as `Processed 127 entries`. Sure, we can log the result every time and append it to a log file of the action logs performed.

We just saw how we can use the CI controller to serve Linux cron services, which has a very powerful capability in many business cases.

Example 1 – default homepage controller

Initially, we will start with a simple controller example that opens a home page with the navigation option back and forth to another page B, and similarly to the home page. We will do so while rendering some controller calculated data at the view.

This example doesn't use the database. This example will be built from the following CI framework component configuration, controller, and view files.

Let us define the default controller filename as `controller/home_page.php` and the home page view as `views/home_page_view.php`.

Let us assume the URI to the project root is `http://mydomain.com/myproject`.

The controller file

The controller file `/home_page.php` will prepare some data to be shown in the view and will let the user navigate to page B and similarly back to the home page.

The helpers used are provided with the sample source code provided with this book.

The following is the code:

```php
<?php
class Home_page extends CI_Controller
{
  function __construct() {
    parent::__construct();
    $this->load->helper ('validators_helper');
    $this->load->helper ('dates_time_helper');
    }
  public function index() {
    $data = array ();
    $data ['email'] = $email = "the@email.com";
    // validators_helpercalls
    $data ['email_valid'] = isValidEmail($email);
    $data ['url'] = $url = "http://cnn.com";
    $data ['url_valid'] = isValidURL($url);
    $data ['url_exist'] = isURLExists($url);
    $this->load->view('home_page_view', $data);
    }
  publicfunction page_b () {
    $data = array ();
    $myqsl_date = "1970-01-01";
    // dates_time_helper calls
```

```
    $data ['since'] = ui_date ($myqsl_date);
    $data ['past'] = getAgeAccurate
        ($myqsl_date, $percision = 2);
    $this->load->view ('page_b_view', $data);
    }
  }
// End controller
```

The view file

The controller file will prepare the current date and time to be shown in the home page views/home_page_view.php view.

```php
<!DOCTYPE html>
<meta content="text/html; charset=utf-8"/>
<?PHP
/* data from controller
$email, $email_valid, $url, $url_valid , $url_exist
*/
$validation_text = ($email_valid) ? "Is Valid ": "Is Not Valid!";
$validation_url = ($url_valid) ? "Is Valid ": "Is Not Valid!";
$exist_url = ($url_exist) ? "Exist ": "Not exist!"; ?>
<body style="text-align: left; color: blue;">
<H1>Main Page</H1>
<HR></HR>
<div style = "float: left">
The Email: <? = $email; ?><? = $validation_text; ?>
</div>
<div style = "clear: both;"></div>
<HR></HR>
<div>
The url: <? = $url; ?><? = $validation_url; ?> and
  <? = $exist_url; ?>
<? = anchor ($url, '[visit the url]', array ("target" => "_blank",
  "title" => "opens a new Tab")); ?>
</div>
<div style = "clear: both;"></div>
<HR></HR>
<?php echo anchor ('home_page/page_b', 'Navigate me to page B') ?>
</body>
</html>
```

The controller has a `page_b()` method to render the following view file. It will prepare the parameters `$since` and `$past` for this page to be used inline in the rendered view `page_b_view`, as follows:

The view file is `views/page_b_view.php`.

```
<!DOCTYPE html>
<meta content="text/html; charset=utf-8" />
<?PHP
/* data from controller $since, $past */ ?>
<body style = "text-align: left; color: blue;">
<H1>Page B</H1>
<HR></HR>
<div style = "float: left">
<!We render the provided controller parameters $since & $past>
Since: <? = $since; ?> past<? = $past; ?> years</div>
<div style = "clear: both;"></div>
<HR></HR>
<?php echo anchor ('home_page', 'Back to Home Page') ?>
</body>
</html>
```

The configuration file

Initially, we shall define at application/config/routes.php the default controller to be called.

```
For example, $route['default_controller'] = "home_page";.
```

So that in case, you will issue URI of the project root in the browser, lets say:

`http://mydomain.com/myproject`

`http://mydomain.com/myproject/home_page will be called.`

Optionally we can configure CI to eliminate the need to use `index.php` as part of the URI path to call our CI project controller/s (Refer for information, to *Chapter 2, Configurations and Naming Conventions*).

Example 2 – sending e-mails with attachments

In this example, we will see how the controller can load a mail service library and use it to send mail attachments.

The CI mail library is not an auto-loaded library, and hence, will be loaded by the controller we are building for sending e-mail.

The CI mail library makes it easy to send subject messages of non-English languages supporting UTF-8 both for the subject and the mail body. Adding attachments to an e-mail becomes a piece of cake using the CI mail library. We only need to have the files on a known directory path in our server and refer to them to attach them to the mail.

We can attach one or more files to create the mail body. HTML/TEXT is defined via a simple configuration setting to the CI mail library.

This example will be constructed from the mail controller only; you may add a rendered view later on to add to the example report on the mailing list, sending a report of a list of e-mail destinations instead of just one or two destinations.

Let us specify the default controller filename as `controller/mail`.

Let us assume the URI to the project root is `http://mydomain.com/myproject`. Hence, the URI to execute the controller for sending the mail will be `http://mydomain.com/myproject/mail`.

We shall remember that in CodeIgniter, if you refer only to the controller URI path, the CI will operate the function controller class `index()` function, if any. In case the controller class does have `index()` function. And actually in any case, the controller constructor will be called to create the class instance.

The controller file

The controller file, `controller/email.php`, will initially load the CI mail library, then it will configure the mail service properties, such as from/to e-mail address, subject, HTML body, and the attachment files. Finally, the controller will issue the e-mail send service of the library, getting back the operation completion status to report to the web user. In case of a failure, the controller will render a report for the reason of the failure with debugging information provided by the CI mail library.

 The helpers used are provided with the sample source code provided with this book.

Since this controller example has several functions, we shall review their usage initially, before we review the code as follows:

- `__construct()`: This contractor loads the CI e-mail library to be used by other functions
- `index()`: This builds the e-mail message and sends it to its destination
- `doc_root_path()`: This provides the directory path to find the e-mail attachments to send

Regarding the need to load resources such as libraries, helpers, and models, the best practice is the amount of usage in our controller. Let's say, for example, that we have 40 controllers and 39 of them need the same library. We shall add that library into the auto-load list, `/config/autoload.php`. If we did add a resource, such as a library, model, or helper into the project auto-load, we can eliminate loading it in the class that needs the resource services as follows:

```php
class Email extends CI_Controller
// The controller/email.php file will contain this class
{
  function __construct()
  {
    // call the parent constructor to inherit all its services
    parent::__construct();
    // Loads the CI e-mail library, so that it will be instantiated
    // and its methods will be accessed, as $this->mail->METHOD_NAME.
    $this->load->library('email');
  }
  // Define the controller methodindex (the default method), so that
  referring to the URI mydomain.com/myproject/email will execute the
  index method call
  function index() {
    // Configure the library to work with UTF-8 strings
    // multi-language support, as well as enable HTML content body.
    $config['charset'] = 'utf-8';
    $config['mailtype'] = 'html';

    // Loads the configuration settings by initialize method
    $this->email->initialize($config);
    // Since the mail body is HTML, define CR/LF to be
    // replaced with HTML <BR/>
    $this->email->set_newline("<BR/>");
    // Define the 'From' Email address
    $this->email->from('eliorr@phpmyqsl.com', 'Eli Orr');
```

```php
// Define the 'To' Email/s
$this->email->to (array('"Name 1" <name1@name.com>',
   '"Name 2" <name2@name.com>'));
// Set the e-mail subject
$this->email->subject
   ("This is the Subject - can be ANY UTF-8 chars");
// Define the e-mail body in HTML format, as we set the message
to be HTML typed
$this->email->message
('<H1>Hello there!<H1/>
<p>
This Email is sent from CI via its cool e-mail library)<BR/>
<font color=green size=3><b>See Attached Files</b></font><BR/>
Attachedfiles: <BR/>
<ul>
<li> 1 - File One.</li>
<li> 2 - Second File </li>
</p>
);


// Load the attachments
$path = $this->doc_root_path ();
// Doc root For example, /home/yourdomain.com/public_html
// Let say attachment under public_html as /attachments
$attachment_path1 = $path."/attachments/file1.jpg";
$attachment_path2 = $path."/attachments/file2.php";


// Set the two attachment file paths
$this->email->attach($attachment_path1);
$this->email->attach($attachment_path2);


// We have the e-mail object ready! Let us send it!
// execute send and check the result status
if ($this->email->send())
{
  // The e-mail was sent successfully.
  echo 'Your email was sent!';
  }
else {
  // We had some problems, let's show what was wrong
  echo $this->email->print_debugger();
  }
}
functiondoc_root_path () {
```

```
    // An auxiliary method for calculating attachment
    // file path in our server
    return $doc_root = $_SERVER["DOCUMENT_ROOT"];
    }
}
```

Example 3 – admin and regular user log in

In this example we will see how the controller can coordinate using models and views a login session for a regular user, as well as an admin super user, so that each will have a distinct menu. In order to use the provided database file and successfully log in, use the following steps:

- For regular user login:
    - ○ User: reg_user
    - ○ Password: 111111111 (9 x 1 s)

- For admin user login:
    - ○ User: admin_user
    - ○ Password: 111111111 (9 x 1 s)

This example will be constructed from the following controller, models, and views:

- application/controller/auth.php: This controller is used to control authentication checkup and redirect each user category to its view or notify of a login failure. Regular users and admin users will have different view menu, message, and logout options.
- application/models/users_model.php: This is the model to validate the submitted user name and password (stored in the database via MD5) against the predefined database table of users.
- application/views/login_view.php: This is the view shown to users that are not logged in, in order to log in.
- application/views/logged_in_view.php: This is the view shown to users that were successfully logged in and performed their roles as reg_user/admin users.
- MySQL database- USERS_DB.sql: This is a database table that we will upload to our database.

Let us assume the URI to the project root is `http://mydomain.com/myproject`.

Hence the URI to execute the auth controller for login will be `http://mydomain.com/myproject/auth`.

The controller file

The controller file, `controller/auth.php`, will initially load the CI form helper; this helper will be used to construct and operate the login form. For more on helper usage and scope, refer to *Chapter 5, Helpers*.

`users_model`, written especially to serve the controller for authenticating users credentials against the user table, will be loaded. The controller `auth/index` will be called from both the initial stage as well as after a `login_view` submission.

The session is a well known issue in PHP and is out of the scope of this book. However, CI enables the storing of operated sessions with served clients via the database in a table named `ci_sessions`.

This way the sessions are much more organized for the project to manipulate with search session and load session parameter. In order to use a database stored session, we shall edit `/config/config.php`.

```
$config['sess_use_database'] = TRUE;
/* Enforce storing sessions data in the database */
```

Also, we will add a session library as we want to use it for this example along with other commonly used `/config/autoload.php` libraries.

```
$autoload['libraries'] = array
   ('database', 'session', 'xmlrpc');
```

In case of a submission, the input post for the password will not be null and the controller will proceed with the credentials checkup using the `users_model` model. If successful, the user record fields will be kept in the session and the controller methods `auth/admin_main_menu` or `auth/user_main_menu` will be called as per the model returned user role. If the logged in user issues the logout anchor, `auth/logout` will be called to destroy the session and redirect the user to the login form.

The following is the code:

```
class Auth extends CI_Controller {
  function __construct() {
    parent::__construct
    $this->load->helper ('form');
    $this->load->model ('users_model');
```

```php
  }
// called with auth is called with no specific method and
// simply calls the login method
function index() {
  $this->login();
  }
functionlogin()
{
  // The message to user in case of login failure
  $msg = "";
  if ($this->input->post('password'))
  {
    // The caller is from the form submission
    // we will check credentials validity using the local method
    // check_login.
    $stat = $this->check_login();
    // Extract failure message to user if any
    $msg = $stat ['msg' ];
    if($stat['result'] == 'ok')
    {
      // Successful login!
      // See what We have
      // admin_user or regular user?
      if ($this->session->userdata ('role') == 'admin_user')
      // Issue the controller for admin user main menu
      redirect('auth/admin_main_menu');
      else
      // Issue regular user main menu controller
      redirect('auth/user_main_menu');
      return;
      }
    }
  else {
    // rendered with no submission
    // let's destroy any previous session and challenge again
    // the user
    $this->session->sess_destroy();
    }
  // We can get here due to login failure or referring to auth
  // controller without any active submission.
  // Keep the msg return from the model into view view_setup
  ['msg'] = $msg;
  // render the login view to challenge the user
  $this->load->view('login_view.php', $view_setup);
  }
```

```php
functioncheck_login() {
    // Extract the credentials from the submitted login_viewform
    $user_name = $this->input->post('user_name');
    $password = $this->input->post('password');
    // init an array to return
    $ret = array ();
    // Check if login is ok and get the $row using the loaded
    // users_model model.
    $user_record = $this->users_model->check_login
      ($user_name, $password);
    if ($user_record) {
        // User passed credentials checkup successfully
        // We have the user record. Let's use it to extract info
        // for the logged session buildup
        $this->session->set_userdata ('user_id', $user_record->id);
        $this->session->set_userdata ('user_name',
          $user_record->user_name);
        $this->session->set_userdata ('role', $user_record->role);
        $ret ['result'] = 'ok'; $ret ['msg' ] = 'Logged-in!';
        }
    else {
    // login failed!
    $ret ['result'] = 'notok';
    // inform the login form to alert user for the failure
    $ret ['msg' ] = 'Invalid User/Pass - Try Again!';
    }
    return $ret;
    }
// logout method called auth/logout
function logout() {
    // destroy the current session
    $this->session->sess_destroy();
    redirect('auth');
    }
functionadmin_main_menu() {
    // Shall render an admin main menu page
    $view_setup ['uid'] = $this->session->userdata ('user_id');
    $view_setup ['user_name'] = $this->session->userdata
      ('user_name');
    $view_setup ['role'] = $this->session->userdata ('role');
    $view_setup ['menu'] = "Add User/Modify User/Delete User";
    $this->load->view ('logged_in_view.php', $view_setup);
    }

functionuser_main_menu() {
    // Shall render a regular user
    $view_setup ['uid'] = $this->session->userdata ('user_id');
```

```
$view_setup ['user_name']= $this->session->userdata
  ('user_name');
$view_setup ['role']= $this->session->userdata ('role');
$view_setup ['menu']= "View Content/Modify Your Account/Logout";
$this->load->view ('logged_in_view.php', $view_setup);
  }
}
```

The model file

The model file `application/models/users_model.php` will serve the controller for authenticating user credentials against the user table. If successful, the model will return the user database row to the caller.

`auth/admin_main_menu` or `auth/user_main_menu` will be called as per the model returned user role. If the logged in user issues the logout anchor, `auth/logout` will be called to destroy the session and redirect the user to the login form.

The following is the code:

```
class Users_model extends CI_Model {
  function __construct()
  {
    parent::__construct();
    }
  functioncheck_login ($user, $pass)
  {
  // Important notice.
  // Since the model extends the base CI model, it already got the
  // instance. However, we can use the $ci = &get_instance(); instead
  // $this-> anywhere in helpers, libraries, and so on.
  // convert the typed password in the login form to md5, same as
  // we do, when opening a user account.
  $md5_pass = md5($pass);
  // build up the query
  $sql = "SELECT * FROM users WHERE user_name = '$user'
  AND password = '$md5_pass' ";
  $q = $this->db->query($sql);
  if ($q->num_rows()) {
    foreach ($q->result() as $row)
    return $row;
    }
  // In case no num_rows: return NULL;
  }
}
```

The database file to upload for this example

We shall upload this database file, provided as part of the book resources, into our database connected to CI.

The user table includes two users, namely `reg_user` and `admin_user`. Their passwords are stored as the md5 of the text passwords, where `111111111` and `222222222` are the passwords of the `reg_user` and `admin_user` users.

The following is the code:

```
-- phpMyAdmin SQL Dump
-- http://www.phpmyadmin.net
SET SQL_MODE="NO_AUTO_VALUE_ON_ZERO";
SET time_zone = "+00:00";
--
-- Table structure for table `users`
--
CREATE TABLE IF NOT EXISTS `users` (
  `id` int(11) NOT NULL AUTO_INCREMENT,
  `user_name` varchar(128) NOT NULL,
  `password` varchar(128) NOT NULL,
  `role` varchar(128) NOT NULL,
  PRIMARY KEY (`id`)
  ) ENGINE=MyISAM DEFAULT CHARSET = utf8 AUTO_INCREMENT = 3;
--
-- Dumping data for table users
--
INSERT INTO `users` (`id`, `user_name`, `password`, `role`)
VALUES (1, 'reg_user', 'bbb8aae57c104cda40c93843ad5e6db8',
  'regular_user'), (2, 'admin_user',
  '0d777e9e30b918e9034ab610712c90cf', 'admin_user');
```

The login_view view file

The `login_view` view is rendered by the `application/auth/index` index method in order to show non-logged in web visitors to a login page, to enable to challenge them with a login stage.

Following a user entering the user name and password and submitting the login_view view form the `application/auth/login` will be called and will check the credentials using the users model. In case of a successful login, and based on the logged in user category fetch from the users model, one of the `auth` methods will be called as follows:

- auth/admin_main_menu: In case the user has the admin role to render the successful login view for the admin user

- auth/user_main_menu: In case the user has the admin role to render the successful login view for the regular user

The view is located at application/views/login_view.php. This view uses many of the CI form helper functions loaded by the auth controller. When a user issues a submission, the input is initially checked at the client side before issuing a submission call to application/auth.

The following is the code:

```
<!DOCTYPE html">
<meta http-equiv = "Content-type" content = "text/html;
  charset=utf-8"/>
<html>
<head>
<script src = http://code.jquery.com/jquery-latest.js
  type = 'text/javascript'></script>
</head>
<body>
<H1>Login Here</H1>
<!—Building the login form using the form helper-->
<?php
// Define the form attributes
// We will use the 'form' helper 'auth' will
// be called on submission only, if check_if_valid()
// will return true!
$submit_attributes = array
  ('onsubmit' =>"return check_if_valid();", 'id' => 'auth');
echoform_open('auth', $submit_attributes);
echo "<table><tr><td>";
// The attributes of the <input tag>
echoform_label("User Name");
echo "</td><td>";
echoform_input(array('name' => 'user_name', 'value' => ''));
echo "</td><td>";

// The error message holders - hidden by default echo
<label id='user_name_err' style = 'color:red; display:none'>
  name is too short </label>";
echo "</td></tr><tr><td>';
echoform_label("Password");
echo "</td><td>";
echoform_password("password","");
echo "</td><td>";
// The error message holders - hidden by default echo
<label id='password_err' style = 'color: red; display: none'>
  password is too short </label>";
```

```
echo "</td></tr>";
echo "</table>";
// The submit button echo
form_input(array('type' => 'submit', 'value' =>'Login'));
echoform_close(); ?>
<HR></HR>
<!-- Server Credentials failure message -->
<p style = "color: red"><?php echo $msg; ?></p>
</body>
<!-- Local JavaScript service -->
<script type='text/javascript'>
functioncheck_if_valid() {
  var submit = true;
  varuser_name = $('[name="user_name"]').val();
  var password = $('[name="password"]').val();
  if (user_name.length< 2) {
    $('#user_name_err').show();
    submit = false;
    }
  else $('#user_name_err').hide();
  if (password.length< 6) {
    $('#password_err').show();
    submit = false;
    }
  else $('#password_err').hide();
  return submit;
  }
</script>
</html>
```

The login_in_view view file

The login_in_view view is rendered following a successful login by either application/auth/admin_main_menu controller method or application/auth/user_main_menu method base on the user category with the info of the logged in user.

Both the controllers uses the users_model model to validate the login attempt and fetch the logged in user. The view shows the logged in user some information about its account, such as the user name and role as well as the menu available for its user category.

The view is located at application/views/login_in_view.php. This view is using parameters provided by the $user_nam, $uid, $role, and $menu controller to be shown to the logged in user. From this view, the user may issue a logout anchor that calls auth/logout to destroy the session and redirect the logged in user to the login view.

Many of the CI form helper functions are loaded by the `auth` controller. When user issues are submitted, the input is initially checked at the client side before issuing a submission call to `application/auth`.

The following is the code:

```
<!DOCTYPE html">
<meta http-equiv = "Content-type" content = "text/html;
  charset<!DOCTYPE html">
<meta http-equiv = "Content-type" content = "text/html;
  charset=utf-8"/>
<html>
<body>
<H1>Welcome <? = $user_name; ?>!</H1>
<H1>You are logged in!</H1>
<HR></HR>
<H3>Your User ID is: <? = $uid; ?></H3>
<H3>Your System Role is:<? = $role; ?></H3>
<H3>Your Menu options: <? = $menu; ?></H3>
<?php echo anchor ('auth/logout', 'Logout') ?>
</body>
</html>
```

Summary

In this chapter, we have reviewed the CI controller scope and the different controller usage categories targeting view rendering and serve AJAX client requests or apache crontab scheduled processing requests. We have reviewed the various resources that the controller can be assisted with, such as the helpers, libraries, and models. Eventually, we have made several usage examples as follows:

- Example 1: default home page controller
- Example 2: sending e-mails with attachments
- Example 3: admin and regular user log in

4
Libraries

This chapter covers the CI libraries topic, and the different types of libraries and their different usage categories, with several code examples of web applications. The CI development platform provides us with the built-in libraries, enables us with an easy procedure to integrate third-party libraries, and also allows us to develop our new libraries and share them with the community, if we wish to.

The CI libraries are powering efficiency, code reusability, separation, and simplicity. The benefits achieved are as follows:

- **Efficiency**: In means of minimal loaded resources. This feature achieved by the fact that the CI library, may be loaded only by the specific CI project controller(s), or even only in specific method(s), where the library's services are required. Hence, the overhead (memory) of the library resources during execution time is minimized in each controller operation state.

- **Reusability**: Reusability means writing once a function code and reusing it across the project resources. The libraries can be loaded by any project controller, model, or helper (in a helper, we shall use the `&get_instance()` method discussed several times before) to reuse their code anywhere in the CI project. More than that, the controller-rendered views can call those loaded library methods. Hence, great code reusability is achieved.

- **Separation**: Separation prevents, accidental overlapping with same name to the parameters or functions elsewhere in the project. The Library class methods and parameters have their own name space so that they can't be overridden by a mistake outside the library in case the developer is using the same parameters in the served module such as controllers/views.

- **Simplicity**: This make the code text as minimal as possible and easy to understand and maintain. The libraries' methods called from the served resources, such as controllers, models, and helpers, make the code look much simpler, and make it easy to maintain and navigate. Hence, this simplifies extending the code and maintaining it.

The libraries give us development power and efficiency with rich-focused functionality on certain project aspects, and also enable us to have simple and concise fashion code in the served controllers by calling the library method, instead of having the service code locally in the controller. The libraries should be initially instantiated by the code using them, such as the controller, model, or helper, or if used by almost all controllers, models can be loaded using the autoload mechanism. *Chapter 2, Configurations and Naming Conventions*, discusses how to autoload the libraries.

Once instantiated by the autoload or controller constructor, the libraries can be used by the controller methods or by rendered views. In addition, any model, helper, or another library may use our project installed libraries using `&get_instance()`, as described in the previous chapters.

The libraries power the code of the CI model-view-controller instantiated components (for more information, visit the website `http://en.wikipedia.org/wiki/Model-view-controller`), regarding the functionality expansion and reusability across the project controllers, models, helpers, and views.

This chapter will primarily focus on the following topics:

- The CI libraries' scope and usage:
    - Usage categories
    - Using a library
    - Adding a library to the project
    - Instantiating a library
    - Using library method(s)
- Available CI libraries
- Examples:
    - Example 1: using the built-in libraries
    - Example 2: using third-party libraries such as the Google Maps CI library wrapper
    - Example 3: building our own library such as the Flickr API wrapper
    - Example 4: building our own library such as the LinkedIn API wrapper

We will begin by briefly reviewing what a library in a CI framework is, and how we can use it for our needs across the project code resources.

The CI libraries' scope and usage

The CI library does not have access to the controller resources by default unless the CI `$ci = &get_instance()` is called and `$ci` is used instead of `$this` to access the CI resources, for example, instead of `$this->db->query ($sql)`, we shall use `$ci->db->query ($sql)`, and so on. We can extend the CI library using the third-party libraries from where CI echo system (the CI community of developers worldwide share knowledge, sources, and solutions for code and open issues), or develop our own libraries from scratch or extending other libraries.

Any application library will be located under `application/libraries/` in the project's directory. In addition, optional resources such as the library configuration file that is required for library configurations can be placed under the project root or elsewhere. A good practice is to place them under the project root for enhanced security provided by CI. For example, `<PROJECT_ROOT>application/config/<LIB_NAME>_config.php`, or even additional resources such as the `images/CSS/HTML/additional` class libraries may be required under another `application/<LIB_ADDITIONAL_RESOURCES>`, such as `application/assets`.

The library integration and the usage within the CI project are as follows:

- Adding the library code resources to `application/libraries/my_lib.php`, optionally adding related resources, if any, such as a library configuration file, and/or other library assets to their locations as mentioned before.

- Instantiating the library class via config autoload, or instantiating it via the controller.

  - Automatically load a library `my_lib` for the entire CI project:

    ```
    $autoload['libraries'] = array('database','my_lib');
    ```

  - Specifically in certain controller(s), constructor(s), or method(s):

    ```
    $this->load->library('my_lib');
    ```

- Using the library methods:

  ```
  $result=$this->my_lib->called_method ($param1, $param2);
  ```

- We can see the library scope as the ultimate OOP reusability enabler for the entire project code resources' models, views, helpers, and libraries, which govern all to address the execution requests from the user, or a scheduled request.

As mentioned, the CI libraries enables us with great Separation and Simplicity. For example, the following code:

```
// Library class
class my_handler {
  private $my_lib_param;
  // Can't be accessed outside the class directly
  // but we can provide the read only service as follows:

  public function get_my_lib_param () {
    return $this->my_lib_param;}
  // The following is a library function that can't
  // be called from outside the class!

  private function my_private_function () { }
}
```

Available CI libraries

CI and the CI echo system of developers provide many libraries covering a rich set of topics. We will review the CI libraries as well as known resources for the third-party CI libraries.

We are also encouraged to build our own libraries that can be used by others, and share them with the community, such as:

- The Git community at https://github.com
- CI Sparks at http://getsparks.org
- CI Forums at http://codeigniter.com/forums
- Packagist at https://packagist.org

To call a built-in library, we shall call for example, the built-in library named CI_Xxxx as follows: $this->load->library (xxxx);. So that CI_ prefix is not used and instead of the capitalized library name Xxxx, we use the lowercase library name xxxx. For calling a library function yyyy within the library **CI_Xxxx**, we shall write $this->xxxx->yyyy();.

The following is a list of built-in and commonly useful CI libraries (As of version 2.1.4):

CI_Benchmark	CI_Encrypt	CI_Migration	CI_Unit_test
CI_Cache	CI_Exceptions	CI_Model	CI_Upload
CI_Cache_apc	CI_Form_validation	CI_Output	CI_URI
CI_Cache_dummy	CI_FTP	CI_Pagination	CI_User_agent
CI_Cache_file	CI_Hooks	CI_Parser	CI_Utf8
CI_Cache_memcached	CI_Image_lib	CI_Profiler	CI_Xmlrpc
CI_Calendar	CI_Input	CI_Router	CI_Xmlrpcs
CI_Cart	CI_Javascript	CI_Security	CI_Zip
CI_Config	CI_Jquery	CI_Session	
CI_Controller	CI_Lang	CI_SHA1	
CI_Driver	CI_Loader	CI_Table	
CI_Driver_Library	CI_Log	CI_Trackback	

In this chapter, we will provide a usage example for Google Maps' third-party library wrapper, available at `https://github.com/ianckc/CodeIgniter-Google-Maps-Library`.

Many more third-party libraries can be found following the CI forums at `http://codeigniter.com/forums`.

Example 1 – using the built-in libraries

In this initial example, we will see how to use the CI built-in library. Here we will use the CI library `CI_Table` as well as the `CI_db` library, which, for a given database table/view and some optional CSS settings, will enable us to render the table nicely with all the HTML table tags and CSS settings in just a single line of code. In this example, we will use the same user's table that we used for the controller example in *Chapter 3*, *Usage and Scope of Controllers*.

This example will be constructed from the following controller and view:

- `application/controllers/builtins.php`: This controller loads the built-in CI library `table` as well as the `db` library, which is autoloaded (for more information, refer to *Chapter 2*, *Configurations and Naming Conventions*) to get the user's table content, and set up the table to render using the `table` library.

```
$this->load->library('table');
```

The controllers prepare vectors of map settings and the list of places and possible controllers to zoom into each of the places, and render a view named `google_map_view`.

- `application/views/users_view.php`: This view will use the `table` library service to render a nicely formatted table as loaded from `db`, and configured by the controller.

 Let us assume that the URL to the project root is `http://mydomain.com/myproject`, `http://mydomain.com/myproject/builtins`. (The source code is provided with this book via URLs.)

The controller file

The following is a step-by-step example of the controller code for each operation:

```php
<?php
/** Use CI built In libraries
class Builtins extends CI_Controller{
  function __construct(){
    parent::__construct();
    // Load the table library that generates the HTML tags for
    // showing the table structure within a view
    $this->load->library('table');
  }
  public function index(){
    // Load the users list from DB into the view
    $data['users'] = $this->db->get('users');
    // Create custom header for the table
    $header = array
    ('id', 'User Name', 'Hashed Password', 'Position' );
    // Set the headings
    $this->table->set_heading($header);
    // Set table formatting
    $table_format = array ( 'table_open'  => '<table border="1"
      cellpadding="2" cellspacing="1" class="mytable">' );
    $this->table->set_template($table_format);
    // Load the view and send the results
    $this->load->view('users_view', $data);
  }
}
```

The view file

To complete the operation, we will finish working on the view file.

```
<!DOCTYPE html">
<meta http-equiv="Content-type" content="text/html;
  charset=utf-8"/>
<html>
<head>
<title>
  Showing Users Table Using CI Build-In table Library
</title>
</head>
<body>
  <div id='results'>
  <!—All The Formatted Table is rendered by the table library
    instance using the controller defined settings and the table
      of users we have fetched from the DB >
  <?php echo $this->table->generate($users); ?>
  </div>
</body>
</html>
```

Example 2 – using third-party libraries such as the Google Maps CI library wrapper

In this example, we will see how to install and use the Google Maps CI library with some cool services. First, we need to download the library files from `http://biostall.com/codeigniter-google-maps-v3-api-library`.

In the downloaded TAR file, we shall find the following libraries:

- `Googlemaps.php`: This is the Google Maps API library for CI. We shall place it at `application/libraries/`.

- `Jsmin.php`: This is an auxiliary code for the library to generate the JavaScript generated code for enabling the smart Google Maps UI interaction. We shall also place it at `application/libraries/`.

- Google Maps V3 API: This is a PDF file for in-depth, possible library settings and usage.

In this example, we will provide an initial page showing several marked places together on the Google Map window that we will create in our application. In that visualized view, we will enable the user to zoom into predefined selected places we have marked on the map using the CI anchor URL helper.

This example will be constructed from the following library, controller, and view:

- `application/libraries/`: This is the CI wrapper library for Google Maps that we downloaded. Refer to the CI library contributor website at `http://biostall.com`.

- `application/controllers/gmaps.php`: This controller loads the `googlemaps` library and builds up several views for several places shown together on the Google Map, and zooms in to each of the places.

  ```
  $this->load->library('googlemaps');
  ```

  The controllers prepare vectors of map settings and the list of places and possible controllers to zoom into each of the places, and render a view named `google_map_view`.

- `application/views/google_map_view.php`: This is the rendered view that initially shows all the places on the Google Map, and lets the user zoom in using a menu option to a listed zoom-in location, or go back to the view of all the places together on a zoom-out map.

Let us assume the URI to the project root is `http://mydomain.com/myproject`. `http://mydomain.com/myproject/gmaps`.

 The source code is provided with this book via URLs.

The controller file

The controller file `controllers/gmaps.php` will initially load the CI Google Maps library, then set up the maps' settings and the places to be marked and shown in different views (the same view file is rendered with different `$data` settings each time). The controller will have the `__construct()` and `index()` methods, in addition to set the zoom in on the defined places.

```php
<?php
/** Use The Google Maps CI Library Wrapper for several
  marked places altogether and zoom-in*/
class Gmaps extends CI_Controller {
  function __construct()
```

```
{  parent::__construct();
  $this->load->library('googlemaps');
  // Set the map window sizes:
  $config['map_width']      = "1000px";
  // map window width
  $config['map_height'] = "1000px";
  // map window height
  $this->googlemaps->initialize($config);
}
function index() {
  /* Initialize and setup Google Maps for our App starting
    with 3 marked places
  London, UK, Bombai, India, Rehovot, Israel
  */
  // Initialize our map for this use case of show 3
  // places altogether.
  // let the zoom be automatically decided by Google for showing
  // the several places on one view.
  $config['zoom'] = "auto";
  $this->googlemaps->initialize($config);
  //Define the places we want to see marked on Google Map!
  $this->add_visual_flag ('London, UK');
  $this->add_visual_flag ('Bombai, India');
  $this->add_visual_flag ('Rehovot, Israel');
  $data = $this->load_map_setting ();
  // Load our view, passing the map data that has just been
  //created.
  $this->load->view('google_map_view', $data);
}
//The class Gmaps continued with several more functions as
//follows:
function london() {
  // Initialize our map
  //Here you can also pass in additional parameters for
  // customizing the map (see the following code:)
  // Define the address we want to be on the map center
  $config['center'] = 'London, UK'; to be on the map center
  // Set Zoom Level - Zoom 0: World – 18 Street Level
  $config['zoom'] = "16";
  $this->googlemaps->initialize($config);
  // Add visual flag
  $this->add_visual_flag ($config['center']);
  $data = $this->load_map_setting ();
  // Load our view passing the map data that has just been
  //created
```

```
      $this->load->view('google_map_view', $data);
   }
   functionBombay() {
   //Initialize our map.
   //Here you can also pass in additional parameters for
   //customizing the map (see the following code)
   //Define the address we want to see as the map center
   $config['center'] = 'Bombay, India';
   $config['zoom'] = "16";   // City Level Zoom
   $this->googlemaps->initialize($config);
   // Add visual flag
   $this->add_visual_flag ($config['center']);
   $data = $this->load_map_setting ();
   // Load our view passing the map data that has just been created
   $this->load->view('google_map_view', $data);
   }
```

The class Gmaps continues with several more functions as follows:

```
   function rehovot()
   {
     // Initialize our map.
     //Here you can also pass in additional parameters for
     //customizing the map (see the following code)
     $config['center'] = 'Rehovot, Israel';
     $config['zoom'] = "16";
     // City Level Zoom
     $this->googlemaps->initialize($config);
     // Add visual flag
     $this->add_visual_flag ($config['center']);
     $data = $this->load_map_setting ();
     // Load our view, passing the map data that has just been
     //created.
     $this->load->view('google_map_view', $data);
   }
   function load_map_setting ( ) {
     $data = array();
     $locations = array();
     $controllers = array();
     // Set controllers list for zoom in
     $locations[] = 'London, UK';
     $locations[] = 'Bombai, India';
     $locations[] = 'Rehovot, Israel';
     // Set controllers list for zoom in
     $controllers[] = "london";
```

```php
    $controllers[] = "bombai";
    $controllers[] = "rehovot";
    $data['map'] = $this->googlemaps->create_map();
    $data['locations'] = $locations;
    $data['controllers'] = $controllers;
    $data['map'] = $this->googlemaps->create_map();
    return $data;
}
```

The class Gmaps continues with several more functions as follows:

```php
function add_visual_flag ( $place ) {
  $marker = array();
  // Setup Marker for the place and the title as the place name
  $marker['position'] = $place;
  $marker['title'] = $place;
  $this->googlemaps->add_marker($marker);
  }
}
```

The view file

The view file will render the provided Google Maps JavaScript and HTML portions as well as render the list of places. It also provides zoom-in and zoom-out navigation options to the places supported by the controller.

```php
<!DOCTYPE html">
<meta http-equiv="Content-type"
content="text/html; charset=utf-8" />
<html>
<head>
  <script src = http://code.jquery.com/jquery-latest.js ></script>
  <!--Render all the map JS provided by rendering controller-->
  <?php echo $map['js']; ?>
</head>
<body>
<H3>CodeIgniter Powered CI Google Maps Library : <H3>
<HR/><ul>
<!—Let the User Always Get Back to the default Zoom out -->
<li><?php  echo anchor("index.php/gmaps",
'<B>See All Locations</B>' ); ?>
</li>
<?PHP
$i=0;
foreach ($locations as $location ) {
```

```
    // Show to the user all the possible Zoom Ins defined places by
    //the controller, so that user may zoom in by issuing the
    // anchor.
    $controller = $controllers["$i"];
    $i++; ?>
    <li>
    <?php echo anchor
    ("index.php/gmaps/$controller", "Zoom-In to ".$location ) ?>
    </li>
    <?PHP } ?>
    }
</ul>
<HR></HR>
<?php echo $map['html']; ?>
</body>
</html>
```

Example 3 – building a library such as the Flickr API wrapper

The flickr.com website by Yahoo! provides API access to the Flickr repository of public photos uploaded to the community. The API is extremely rich, and its documentation is available at http://www.flickr.com/services/api/, and is called **App Garden**.

The API is enabled for various programming languages and access methods. We will build a solution of a wrapper that can be expanded to get any Flickr API service, using the PHP REST access method.

This example will be constructed from the following library, controller, and view:

- application/libraries/flickr_wrapper.php: The is the CI wrapper library that enables smooth Flickr API access via CI. This basic services library can be expanded to support the entire Flickr App Garden.

- application/controllers/flickr_recent.php: This is the controller that uses the flickr_wrapper library that we wrote and pulls the recent public photos uploaded with the EXIF photo info and the photographer-related information.

- application/views/flickr_recent_view.php: This is the view that shows the collected information of recent photos and photographers.

Let us assume the URI to the project root is `http://mydomain.com/myproject`. Hence, the URI to execute the auto controller for logging in will be `http:// mydomain.com/myproject/flickr_recent`.

The flickr_wrapper.php library file

The `application/libraries/flickr_wrapper.php` library file contains the library `flickr_wrapper` class library that we are building and using to access the Flickr App Garden API. It is mandatory to load this library with a valid Flickr `api_key` that you can get by following the Flickr App Garden documentation. The library will use the PHP REST API access, so that we can later expand any of the Flickr API services to be supported with our library. Each of the library methods returns a multidimensional keyed array of the resultant data.

The following is the code:

```
/**
 * CodeIgniter Flickr API wrapper Library Class
 *
 * Enable Simple Flickr API usage
 *
 * @package         CodeIgniter
 * @category    Libraries
 * @author          Eli Orr
 * Usage:
 * Via CI controller:
 * $this->load->library( 'flickr_wrapper',
 * array(   'api_key'       => '<YOUR_FLICKR_API_KEY>',
 * 'DEFAULT_RES' => '3000',
// filter 3000 pix
 * 'GPS_ENABLED' => FALSE ));
 * $this->flickr_wrapper->set_params ( $keyed_array );
 * $recent_photos =
 * $this->flickr_wrapper->flickrPhotosGetRecent ();
 * $filter_photos =
 * $this->flickr_handler->
 * filter_photos ($photos_to_filter);
 * $user_info         =
 * $this->flickr_wrapper->flickrUserInfo ($uid);
 * // $uid e.g. 72095130@N00
//.PRIVATE
//We will use the following private functions:
private function _file_get_contents_curl($url);
private function _flickrRestAPI ($params);
private function _is_filtered_photo ($photo_rec );
 */
```

The following is the `Flickr_wrapper` class that we are building:

```
class Flickr_wrapper {
  // parameters as part of the library instance
  private $DEFAULT_RES = 2000;
  // Width in Pixels
  private $GPS_ENABLED = TRUE;
  // total shown photos
  private $RECENT_PHOTOS = 500;
  // how many photos in each poll ?
  // CI instance
  private $CI;
  // Flickr api_key to use
  private $api_key = "" ;
  function __construct( $params = array())
  {
    // Make sure we got the api_key - otherwise exit!
    if (!isset ($params['api_key']))
    exit ('FATAL - must be constructed with api_key!');
    $this->set_params ($params);
    // Just for debugging needs, we may drop those later
    error_reporting(E_ALL);
    ini_set('display_errors', '1');
  }
  // change settings on the fly
  function set_params ( $key_array ) {
    // sets array of instance parameters
    foreach ($key_array as $key => $val ){
      switch ($key) {
        case 'DEFAULT_RES': $this->DEFAULT_RES   = $val; break;
        case 'GPS_ENABLED': $this->GPS_ENABLED   = $val; break;
        case 'RECENT_PHOTOS': $this->RECENT_PHOTOS = $val; break;
      case 'api_key' : $this->api_key = $val; break;
      // We can add many more here.
        default: exit ("FATAL! - set_params invalid param: $key");
    }
  }
}
}
```

The class code continues while shifting our focus on accessing the recent public photos.

```
// Pulls recent public photos as multi-dimensional array
function flickrPhotosGetRecent () {
  #
```

```
    # build the Params for API
    #
    $params = array(
        'api_key' => $this->api_key,
        'method' => 'flickr.photos.getRecent',
        'extras' => 'o_dims,owner_name,date_taken,media,
        path_alias,url_sq,geo',
        'per_page' => $this->RECENT_PHOTOS,
        'format' => 'php_serial'
    );
    $rsp_obj = $this->_flickrRestAPI ($params);
    #
    # check if ok or successful result :
    #
    if ($rsp_obj['stat'] == 'ok') {
        # Get the array of all the photo records in this cycle
        return $recent_photos = $rsp_obj['photos']['photo'];
    }
    else
    # Query failed we shall return NULL to the caller
    return NULL;
}
// Get the Photo EXIF that has a lot of info related to the
// photo for a given photo id
```

The class code continues, where we will see how to access additional information related to the image.

```
function GetPhotoExif ($photo_id) {
    #
    # build the API URL to call
    #
    $params = array(
        'api_key' => $this->api_key,
        'method' => 'flickr.photos.getExif',
        'photo_id' => $photo_id,
        'format' => 'php_serial',
    );
    $rsp_obj = $this->_flickrRestAPI ($params);
    #
    # display the photo title (or an error if it failed)
    #
    if ($rsp_obj['stat'] == 'ok') {
        /*
        Array ([photo] => Array ([id] => 8002716747
```

```
    [secret] => 559f87aea0
  [server] => 8030
  [farm] => 9
  [camera] => Casio EX-H20G
  [exif] => ... A LOT OF EXTRA INFO
  */

  $photo_camera = $rsp_obj['photo']['camera'];
  // We can add more interesting items for our app here
  $params = array
  ( 'camera'    => $photo_camera,
  'full_exif' => $rsp_obj
  // All EXIF info for the photo_id
  );
  return $params;
  }
  else // Request Failed We shall return error:
  return NULL;
}
```

Let's see how we can apply photo filtering with the following code:

```
// apply photos filtering on a provided photos array
// based on the current settings
function filter_photos ($photos) {
  $filtered_photos = array();
  foreach ($photos  as $photo) {
    if ($this->_is_filtered_photo ($photo) )
    $filtered_photos[] = $photo;
  }
  return $filtered_photos;
}
function flickrUserInfo ($uid) {
  // UID e.g. : 72095130@N00
  // find info for this User
  #
  # build the API URL to call
  #
  $params = array(
    'api_key'    => $this->api_key,
    'method'     => 'flickr.people.getInfo',
    'user_id'    => $uid,
    'extras'     => 'contact,friend,family',
    'format'     => 'php_serial',
  );
```

```
$rsp_obj = $this-> _flickrRestAPI ($params);
#
# Check if response is OK
#
if ($rsp_obj['stat'] == 'ok'){
  // Yes! We have a good result .. let's load it to the
  // keyed array structure
  $real_name =
  @urlencode($rsp_obj['person']['realname']['_content']);
  $location = @urlencode
  (strtolower ($rsp_obj['person']['location']['_content']));
  $photos = @$rsp_obj['person']['photos']['count']['_content'];
  // more can be added
```

The class code continues as follows:

```
    $params = array (
      'name' => $real_name,
      'uid' => $uid,
      'photos' => $photos,
      'location' => $location,
      'full_info' => $rsp_obj
    );
    return $params;
  }
  else // Response failed return NULL
  return NULL;
}
// PRIVATE SECTION OF ALL PRIVATE LIBRARY METHODS
// THAT CANNOT BE CALLED DIRECTLY FROM THE LIBRARY USER
// This is the heart of our wrapper library that makes it easy to get
// The Flickr API access via simple keyed array based calls and
response
private function _flickrRestAPI ($params) {
  $encoded_params = array();
  foreach ($params as $k => $v){
    $encoded_params[] = urlencode($k).'='.urlencode($v);
  }
  #
  # call the API and decode the response
  #
  $url = "http://api.flickr.com/services/rest/?".implode
  ('&', $encoded_params);
  // This will create get query URI ...?param1=val1&param2=val2
  // and so on
```

```
        $rsp = $this->_file_get_contents_curl($url);
        return $rsp_obj = unserialize($rsp);
    }
```

The class code continues as follows:

```
    // This function assure we can get a url content into a buffer
    // it requires that a PHP curl library is installed!
    private function _file_get_contents_curl($url) {
        if (! function_exists('curl_init') )
        exit ('PHP curl library is not enabled please fix!');
        $ch = curl_init();
        curl_setopt($ch, CURLOPT_HEADER, 0);
        curl_setopt($ch, CURLOPT_RETURNTRANSFER, 1);
        curl_setopt($ch, CURLOPT_URL, $url);
        $data = curl_exec($ch);
        curl_close($ch);
        return $data;
    }
    private function _is_filtered_photo ($photo_rec ) {
        /*
        [o_width]   => 4416
        [latitude] => 0
        //More can be added
        */
        // Photo width  shall be larger than  $this->DEFAULT_RES ?
        if (    (int) (@$photo_rec['o_width'] )  <
        (int)  $this->DEFAULT_RES )          return FALSE;
        // GPS info required & Found ?
        if (( $this->GPS_ENABLED && ! @$photo_rec['latitude'] ))
        return FALSE;
        // if we are here the filtered photo passed successfully
        return TRUE;
        }
    }
```

The flickr_recent.php controller file

The `application/controllers/flickr_recent.php` controller file will load the `flickr_wrapper` API, call its services for newly uploaded public photos and photographers, and render a view to show the results.

In order to execute the controller, you should point your browser to the following URI: `http://mydomain.com/myproject/flickr_recent`.

The following is the controller code:

```php
<?php
/**
 * Flickr Recent Controller
 *
 * Provide recent uploaded public photos in flickr community
 * Enable to apply several settings and filtering
 * Enable to get photographer user profile for each photo
 *
 * @author Eli Orr
 */
class Flickr_recent extends CI_Controller{
  function __construct()
  {
    parent::__construct();
    /*
    Standard Libraries, database, & helper url are included in the
    configs/autoload.php
    */
    // This lines are only for debugging needs we may drop them
    // if things are going good
    error_reporting(E_ALL);
    ini_set('display_errors', '1');
    /* ------Loading User Defined Library------------ */
    $this->load->library
    ( 'flickr_wrapper',
    array('api_key' => '<YOUR_FLICKR_API>',
    'DEFAULT_RES' => '3000',
    // filter 3000 pix
    'GPS_ENABLED' => FALSE
    )
    );
  }
```

The class code continues as follows:

```php
function index () {
  $settings = array(
    'DEFAULT_RES' => '4000',  // Only 4000 pix and better
    'GPS_ENABLED' => FALSE,  // GPS Info is not mandatory
    'RECENT_PHOTOS' => 50,  // Latest 100 photo uploads
  );
  $this->flickr_wrapper->set_params ( $settings );
  $photos_to_filter =
```

```
$this->flickr_wrapper->flickrPhotosGetRecent ();
$filter_photos =
$this->flickr_wrapper->filter_photos ($photos_to_filter);
$data = Array();
$data['photos'] = $filter_photos;
$data['settings'] = $settings;
$this->load->view('flickr_recent_view.php',$data );
  }
}
```

The flickr_recent_view.php view file

The `flickr_recent_view.php` view file is rendered by our controller named `Flickr_recent` defined previously. This controller uses our developed `flickr_wrapper` library in order to get the recent Flickr uploaded photos with their associated information.

The view file is located at `application/views/flickr_recent_view.php`. This view uses the CI parser for the PHP inserted parameters using the `<?=$param ?>` notation.

The following is the code:

```
<!DOCTYPE html>
<html>
<head>
<meta charset="UTF-8" />
<div>
<H1>Flickr Recent Uploads</H1>
<p>
<!-- Show the applied filter settings first -->
<table border="1" style='background-color:#b0c4de;' >
<tr>
  <td>Photos in Poll</td><td><?=$settings['RECENT_PHOTOS'];?></td>
</tr>
<tr>
  <td>Min. Width Filter</td><td><?=$settings['DEFAULT_RES'];
    ?>Px</td>
</tr>
<tr>
  <td>GPS Filter</td><td><?=$settings['GPS_ENABLED']
    ? "With GPS" : "With/Without GPS"; ?></td>
</tr>
</p>
<!-- For each photo show the User name, how many photos they took
```

```
till now, the original size in MP (Mega Pixels)
of the photos and the Time stamp when the photo was taken by the
camera (mostly loaded days or even weeks/months later)
<table border="1"  style='background-color:#009900;'  >
<tr>
  <th>User Uploaded</th><th>User photos Count</th>
  <th>Photo ID</th><th>Original Size MP</th><th>Was Taken</th>
</tr>
```

The class code continues as follows:

```php
<?PHP foreach($photos as $photo )
{
  // get the owner id
  $uid = $photo['owner'];
  // Get User Info
  $user_info = $this->flickr_wrapper->flickrUserInfo ($uid);
  $photos = number_format ($user_info["photos"]);
  $mp_res = (int) ((( $photo['o_width' ] * $photo['o_height'] )
    / 1000000)  +  1);
  ?>
  <tr>
    <td> <?=$photo['ownername'] ?></td>
    <td> <?=$photos ?></td>
    <td> <?=$photo['id'] ?></td>
    <td> <?=$mp_res ?></td>
    <td> <?=$photo['datetaken'] ?></td>
  </tr>
  <?PHP        } ?>
  </table>
</div>
</body>
</html>
```

Example 4 – the LinkedIn API wrapper

In this example, we will build the CI Library wrapper to integrate with the LinkedIn API in order to query the LinkedIn information from it.

There are several challenges in doing so, one of which is to get the token to access the LinkedIn resources and access the data objects such as the following:

- The LinkedIn user's details
- The LinkedIn user's connections

- The LinkedIn company's details
- The LinkedIn company's updates

Requirements

- The PHP extension `oauth` library must be installed from `http://il1.php.net/manual/en/book.oauth.php`.

- We shall register the application at LinkedIn Developers Network Homepage to receive the API key from `http://developer.linkedin.com`. This unique API key is required to identify our application in order to grant access from LinkedIn for responding to our API calls to their API. Once we've registered our LinkedIn app, we will be provided with an API key and a secret key. For the safety of our application, we do not share our secret key. For more information, please refer to `http://developer.linkedin.com/`.

Authentication flowchart

The following steps are required to authenticate our LinkedIn application to grant access. We will refer to this project as LinkedIn app.

1. The LinkedIn API client sends a request to LinkedIn. The client sends the request to the LinkedIn request token URL at `https://api.linkedin.com/uas/oauth/requestToken` via the `oauth` object with a `callback URL` as a parameter to the LinkedIn API. The `callback URL` parameter is the URL to return to from the LinkedIn Authorization URL, where the LinkedIn user shall confirm the LinkedIn app's required permission. The LinkedIn server responds and returns the `oauth` token (public key) and the `ouath` token secret key.

   ```
   Client > Server request token URL
   parameter: callback URL < Server returns oauth token, ouath token
   secret
   ```

2. The client sends the request to the LinkedIn server auth URL using the `oauth_token` token received from `https://api.linkedin.com/uas/oauth/authorize ?oauth_token = oauth_token`, where `oauth_token` is the oauth token returned from the server at phase 1.

   ```
   Client > Server auth URL
   $_GET parameter: oauth token
   ```

3. The LinkedIn server returns the oauth token, the oauth token secret, and the `oauth_verifier` to the client.

```
Client < Server
oauth token, oauth token secret, oauth_verifier
```

4. The client sends the request to the LinkedIn Server access token path at `https://api.linkedin.com/uas/oauth/accessToken`.

```
Client > Server access token path
parameter: oauth_verifier (from phase 2) < Server returns
    oauth token, ouath token secret
```

This example will be constructed from the following controller, library, and view:

- `application/controllers/linkedinfo.php`: The controller that uses the LinkedIn library for authentication and displaying the output returned by the library

- `application/libraries/linkedin_handeler.php`: The `linkedin_handler` library, which enables access to the LinkedIn resources, such as the LinkedIn user's details and connections, and the companies' details

- `application/views/linkedin-me.php`: The view, which displays the LinkedIn user's details

- `application/views/linked-connections.php`: The view, which displays the LinkedIn user's connections

- `application/views/linked-company.php`: The view, which displays the company's details

- `application/views/linked-company-updates.php`: The view, which displays a company's updates

Let us assume the URI to the project root is `http://mydomain.com/myproject`.

Hence, the URI to execute the auth controller for login will be `http://mydomain.com/myproject/linkedinfo`.

The linkedin_handler.php library file

The library file `application/libraries/linkedin_handler.php` contains the class library `linkedin_handler`.

The library contains the function for authenticating the app and accessing the LinkedIn resources.

The following is the code:

```php
<?php

if (!defined('BASEPATH')) exit('No direct script access allowed');

// The php oauth extension is required
// For more information refer to
// http://il1.php.net/manual/en/book.oauth.php
if(!extension_loaded('oauth')) {
    throw new Exception('Simple-LinkedIn: library not compatible with
        installed PECL oauth extension. Please disable this extension to
        use the Simple-LinkedIn library.');
}
/*
 *    CodeIgniter LinkedIn API
 *
 *    @package CodeIgniter
 *
 *    @author  Yehuda Zadik
 *
 *
 *    Enable Simple LinkedIn API usage
 */
class Linkedin_handler {
    const LINKEDIN_API_URL = 'https://api.linkedin.com';

    private $api_key;
    private $secret_key;
    private $on_failure_url;

    // Oauth class
    public $oauth_consumer;

    // The url to return to from LinkedIn
    // authorize url in our case is
    // http://mydomain.com/return_from_provider
```

```php
private $callback_url;

// The request token URL
private $request_token_url;

// LinkedIn authorize URL for getting the LinkedIn user
// confirmation for required permissions
private $authorize_path;

// LinkedIn URL for getting the tokens to access
// the LinkedIn URL resources
private $access_token_path;

// accessory variable for accessing the LinkedIn resources
private $api_url;

// CI instance
private $CI;

/*
 *  Set the class variables
 */
private function set_varaiables() {
  $this->request_token_url = self::LINKEDIN_API_URL .
    '/uas/oauth/requestToken';
  $this->authorize_path = self::LINKEDIN_API_URL .
    '/uas/oauth/authorize';
  $this->access_token_path = self::LINKEDIN_API_URL .
    '/uas/oauth/accessToken';

  $this->api_url = array('people' =>
    'http://api.linkedin.com/v1/people/~' , 'connections' =>
      'http://api.linkedin.com/v1/people/~/connections',
        'companies' => 'http://api.linkedin.com/v1/companies/');

  $this->CI = &get_instance();
  }
/*
 *  Library constructor
 *
 *  Initializes the library variables
 *  and initializes oauth consumer object
 *
 *  @param $config array of the Linked configuration variables
 */
```

```php
    public function __construct($config) {
      // Setting the handler's variables;
      foreach ($config as $k => $v) {
        $this->$k = $v;
        }

      // Setting all the class variables
      $this->set_varaiables();

      // Initializing the oauth consumer object
      $this->oauth_consumer = new oauth($this->api_key,
        $this->secret_key);

      // Enabling Oauth debug
      $this->oauth_consumer->enableDebug();

      // Checking if returned from the LinkedIn UI permission
      // conformation window
      if ($this->CI->input->get('oauth_verifier') ||
        $this->CI->input->get('oauth_problem')) {
        $this->on_success();
        } elseif (!$this->CI->session->userdata('oauth_token')
      && !$this->CI->session->userdata('oauth_token_secret')) {
        // if session variables are not set: oauth_token,
        // oauth_token_secret
        // call auth to start the process of getting the tokens from
        // LinkedIn via the oauth consumer object
        $this->auth();
        } elseif ($this->CI->session->userdata('oauth_token')
      && $this->CI->session->userdata('oauth_token_secret')) {
        // if session variables are set: oauth_token,
        // oauth_token_secret initialize the oauth consumer with
        // $oauth_token, $oauth_token_secret
        $oauth_token = $this->CI->session->userdata('oauth_token');
        $oauth_token_secret = $this->CI->session->userdata
          ('oauth_token_secret');

        // initialize oauth consumer with $oauth_token,
        // $oauth_token_secret
        $this->setToken($oauth_token, $oauth_token_secret);
        }
    }
  /*
   * Start the process of getting oauth token & oauth token
   * secret so that the user
   * redirects to a LinkedIn UI permission conformation window
```

```
*/
public function auth()  {
  // Start communication with the LinkedIn server
  $request_token_response = $this->getRequestToken();

  $this->CI->session->set_userdata('oauth_token_secret',
    $request_token_response['oauth_token_secret']);

  // Get the token for the LinkedIn authorization url
  $oauth_token = $request_token_response['oauth_token'];

  $log_message = 'yuda auth getRequestToken oauth_token: : ' .
    $oauth_token;
  $log_message = "oauth_token_secret: " .
    $request_token_response['oauth_token_secret'] . "\n";
  log_message('debug', $log_message) ;

  // Redirect to the LinkedIn authorization url for getting
  // permissions for the app
  header("Location: " . $this->generateAuthorizeUrl($oauth_token));
  }
/*
 * This is the method called after returning
 * from the LinkedIn authorization URL
 * The returned values from the LinkedIn authorization URL are:
 * oauth_token, oauth_token_secret, oauth_verifier
 * Those values are used to retrieve oauth_token,
 * oauth_token_secret for accessing the LinkedIn resources
 *
 */
public function on_success() {
  if ($this->CI->input->get('oauth_problem')) {
    redirect($this->on_failure_url);
    }

  // Set the oauth consumer tokens
  $this->setToken($this->CI->input->get('oauth_token'),
    $this->CI->session->userdata('oauth_token_secret'));

  // Sending request to the LinkedIn access_token_path to
  // receive the array, which it's keys are tokens: oauth_token,
  // oauth_token_secret for accessing the LinkedIn resources
  $access_token_reponse = $this->getAccessToken
    ($this->CI->input->get('oauth_verifier'));
```

```
     // Setting the session variables with the tokens: oauth_token,
     // oauth_token_secret for accessing the LinkedIn resources
     $this->CI->session->set_userdata('oauth_token',
       $access_token_reponse['oauth_token']);
     $this->CI->session->set_userdata
       ('oauth_token_secret',$access_token_reponse
         ['oauth_token_secret']);

     // Redirecting to the main page
     redirect('');
     }

 /*
  * This method sends the request token to LinkedIn
  *
  * @return array keys: oauth_token, oauth_token_secret
  */
 public function getRequestToken() {
   // The LinkedIn request token url
   $request_token_url = $this->request_token_url;

   // The LinkedIn app permissions
   $request_token_url =
     "?scope = r_basicprofile+r_emailaddress+r_network";

   // Getting the response from the LinkedIn request token URL.
   // The method returns the response, which is an array
   // with the following keys: oauth_token, oauth_token_secret
   return $this->oauth_consumer->getRequestToken
     ($request_token_url, $this->callback_url);
   }
 /*
  * This method returns the LinkedIn authorize URL
  *
  * @param $oauth_token string oauth token for the LinkedIn
  * authorzation URL
  *
  * @return string URL of the LinkedIn authorization URL
  */
 public  function generateAuthorizeUrl($oauth_token) {
   return $this->authorize_path . "?oauth_token = " .
     $oauth_token;
   }
 /*
  * This method sets the token and secret keys of
```

```
 * the oauth object of the oauth protocol
 *
 * @param $oauth_token string oauth token
 * @param $oauth_token_secret oauth_token_secret
 *
 */
public function setToken($oauth_token, $oauth_token_secret) {
  $this->oauth_consumer->setToken($oauth_token,
    $oauth_token_secret);
  }
/*
 * This method requests the LinkedIn tokens for
 * accessing the LinkedIn resources
 * It returns an array with the following keys: oauth_token,
 * oauth_token_secret
 *
 * @param $oauth_verifier string
 *
 * @return array Array with the following keys:
 *   oauth_token, oauth_token_secret,
 * which are used to access the LinkedIn resources URL
 */
public function getAccessToken($oauth_verifier) {
  try {
    // Returns an array with the following keys:
    // oauth_token, oauth_token_secret
    // These keys are used to access the LinkedIn
    // resources URL
    return $this->oauth_consumer->getAccessToken
      ($this->access_token_path, '', $oauth_verifier);
    } catch(OAuthException $E) {
    echo "<pre>";var_dump($this->oauth_consumer);
    echo "</pre><br><br>";
    echo "Response: ". $E->lastResponse;
    exit();
    }
  }
/*
 * This function returns a LinkedIn user's details
 * It returns a JSON string containing these values
 *
 * @return $json string String containing user's details
 */
public function me() {
  $params = array();
```

```
$headers = array();
$method = OAUTH_HTTP_METHOD_GET;
$api_url = $this->api_url['people'] . '?format = json';

try {
  // Request for a LinkedIn user's details
  $this->oauth_consumer->fetch
    ($api_url, $params, $method, $headers);

  // Receiving the last response with json
  // containing the user's details
  $s_json = $this->oauth_consumer->getLastResponse();
  return $s_json;
  } catch(OAuthException $E) {
  echo "<pre>";var_dump($this->oauth_consumer);
  echo "</pre><br><br>";
  echo "Response: ". $E->lastResponse;
  exit();
  }
}
/*
* This function returns a LinkedIn user's connections
* It returns a JSON string containing these values
*
* @return $json string String containing user's connections
*/
public function connections() {
  $params = array();
  $headers = array();
  $method = OAUTH_HTTP_METHOD_GET;
  $api_url = $this->api_url['connections'] .
    '?count = 10&format = json';

  try {
    // Request for a LinkedIn user's connections
    $this->oauth_consumer->fetch
      ($api_url, $params, $method, $headers);

    // Receiving the last response with json containing the user's
    // connections
    $s_json = $this->oauth_consumer->getLastResponse();
    return $s_json;
    } catch(OAuthException $E) {
    echo "<pre>";var_dump($this->oauth_consumer);
    echo "</pre><br><br>";
```

```
      echo "Response: ". $E->lastResponse;
      exit();
      }
   }
/*
 * This function returns a LinkedIn company' details
 * It returns a JSON string containing these values
 *
 * @param Integer $company_id - company id
 *
 * @return $json string String containing a company' details
 */
public function company($company_id) {
  $params = array();
  $headers = array();
  $method = OAUTH_HTTP_METHOD_GET;
  $api_url = $this->api_url['companies'] . $company_id;

  // The following company's details are required:
  // company_id, number of employees, foundation year,
  // number of the company's followers
  $api_url = ':(id, name, website-url, twitter-id,
    employee-count-range, specialties, founded-year,
      num-followers)?format = json';

  try {
    // Request for a LinkedIn company's details
    $this->oauth_consumer->fetch
      ($api_url, $params, $method, $headers);

    // Receiving the last response with json containing the
    // company's details
    $s_json = $this->oauth_consumer->getLastResponse();
    return $s_json;
    } catch(OAuthException $E) {
    echo "<pre>";var_dump($this->oauth_consumer);
    echo "</pre><br><br>";
    echo "Response: ". $E->lastResponse;
    exit();
    }
  }
/*
 * This function returns a LinkedIn company' three updates
 * It returns a JSON string containing these values
 *
```

```
  * @param Integer $company_id - company id
  *
  * @return $json string String containing company's three updates
  */
public function company_updates($company_id) {
  $params = array();
  $headers = array();
  $method = OAUTH_HTTP_METHOD_GET;
  $api_url = $this->api_url[ 'companies'] .
    $company_id . '/updates?start = 0 & count = 3 & format = json';

  try {
    // Request for a LinkedIn company's three updates
    $this->oauth_consumer->fetch
      ($api_url, $params, $method, $headers);

    // Receiving the last response with json
    // containing company's three updates
    $s_json = $this->oauth_consumer->getLastResponse();
    return $s_json;
    } catch(OAuthException $E) {
    echo "<pre>"; var_dump($this->oauth_consumer);
    echo "</pre><br><br>";
    echo "Response: ". $E->lastResponse;
    exit();
    }
  }
}
// Class closing tags
/*  End of file linkedin.php */
/* Location: ./application/libraries/linkedin_handler.php */
```

The linkedinfo.php controller file

The controller file `application/controllers/linkedinfo.php` will load
the LinkedIn API, call its services, and render a view to show the results.

The following is the controller code:

```php
<?php
if (!defined('BASEPATH')) exit('No direct script access allowed');

/**
 * *
 * The controller is loading our developed library
```

```
 * LinkedIn (wrapper)
 * Next, the following process will occur in the loaded library.
 * 1 - get oauth token & oauth token secret so that the user
 * will be redirected to a LinkedIn UI permission conformation
 * window to approve our requested permission.
 * 2 - If user confirms the permissions we requested,
 * the method onSuccess is called with the
 * oauth token & oauth token secret as $_GET parameters.
 * The tokens will be stored as session parameters.
 * Else we cannot proceed querying LinkedIn and the onFailure.
 *
 * Now we can access the LinkedIn resources using the retrieved
.*.tokens.
 * Here are the methods that query LinkedIn resources:
 * me() - Get the Info of the User who confirmed the permissions
 * connections() - Get the preceding user connection records JSON
 * formatted
 * company() - We just gave an example how to retrieve any company
 * by company id we got from the results or query company
 * id by company id or search criteria
 * company_updates() - Let us get the latest updates of this
 * company
 */
class Linkedinfo extends CI_Controller {
  // array of LinkedIn configuration variables
  private $linkedin_config;

  // callback url from the LinkedIn authorization URL
  private $callback_url;
  /*
   * Controller constructor
   *
   * Checks if session variables are set: oauth_token,
   * oauth_token_secret
   * If they are set, then it initializes the oauth consumer
   * else it will call the method auth() to start the
   * process of setting the token
   * It also loads the LinkedIn library
   */
  public function __construct() {

    parent::__construct();

    $linked_config = array(
      // Application keys registered in the
      // LinkedIn developer app
```

```php
      <api_key> => <esq76cosbm9x>,
        <secret_key> => <TyUQ2FzRRzWz9bHk>,
        // The url to return from the
        // LinkedIn confirmation URL
        <callback_url> => base_url() . <linkedinfo/on_success>,
        // The URL when the failure occurs
          <on_failure_url> => <linkedinfo/on_failure>);


    // Load the LinkedIn library
    $this->load->library(<linkedin_handler>,
      $linked_config);
    }
  /*
   * Load the main menu of the application
   */
  public function index() {
    $this->load->view(<linkedin-menu>);
    }
  /*
   * This is the method called after returning
   * from the LinkedIn authorization URL
   * The returned values from the LinkedIn authorization URL are:
   * oauth_token, oauth_token_secret, oauth_verifier
   * Those values are used to retrieve oauth_token,
   * oauth_token_secret for accessing the LinkedIn resources
   *
   *
   */
  public function onSucess() {
    // Set the oauth consumer tokens
    $this->linkedin->setToken($this->input->get(<oauth_token>),
      $this->session->userdata(<oauth_token_secret>));


    // Sending the request to the LinkedIn access_token_path to
    // receive the array, which it's keys
    // are tokens: oauth_token, oauth_token_secret for
    // accessing the LinkedIn resources
    $access_token_reponse = $this->linkedin->getAccessToken
      ($this->input->get('oauth_verifier'));


    // Setting the session variables with the tokens: oauth_token,
    // oauth_token_secret for accessing the LinkedIn resources
    $this->session->set_userdata(<oauth_token>,
      $access_token_reponse[<oauth_token>]);
    $this->session->set_userdata(<oauth_token_secret>,
      $access_token_reponse[<oauth_token_secret>]);
```

```
  // Redirecting to the main page
  redirect(<>);
  }
/*
 *
 */
/*
 * This function calls the library method me to get
 * the LinkedIn user>s details
 */
public function me() {
  // Get the LinkedIn user>s details
  $s_json = $this->linkedin->me();
  $o_my_details = json_decode($s_json);
  $prodile_url =
    $o_my_details->siteStandardProfileRequest->url;

  $view_params[<my_details>] = $o_my_details;
  $view_params[<profile_url>] = $prodile_url;

  // Load the view for displaying the LinkedIn user>s details
  $this->load->view(<linkedin-me>, $view_params);
  }
/*
 * This function calls the library method me to get
 * the LinkedIn user>s connections
 */
public function connections() {
  // Get the LinkedIn user>s connections
  $s_json = $this->linkedin->connections();
  $o_json = json_decode($s_json);

  // Processing data received from the LinkedIn library
  $a_connections = array();
  for ($index = 0; $index < $o_json->_count; $index++) {
    if ($o_json->values[$index]->id == <private>) {
      continue;
      }

    if (isset($o_json->values[$index]->pictureUrl)) {
      $picture_url = $o_json->values[$index]->pictureUrl;
      } else {
      $picture_url = <> ;
```

```
            }

        $a_connections[] = array(‹picture_url› => $picture_url,
          ‹name› => $o_json->values[$index]->firstName .
            « «. $o_json->values[$index]->lastName,
              ‹headline› => $o_json->values[$index]->headline,
                ‹industry› => $o_json->values[$index]->industry,
                  ‹url› => $o_json->values
                    [$index]->siteStandardProfileRequest->url);
        }


    $view_params[‹connections_count›] = $o_json->_total;
    $view_params[‹connections›] = $a_connections;


    // Load the view for displaying the LinkedIn user›s
    // connections
    $this->load->view(‹linked-connections›, $view_params);
    }
/*
 * This function the calls library method me to get
 * the LinkedIn company›s details
 *
 * @param $company_id integer - Linkedin company id
 */
public function companies($company_id) {
    // Get the LinkedIn company›s details
    $s_json = $this->linkedin->company($company_id);
    $o_company_details = json_decode( $s_json);

    $a_company_details = array (‹id› => $company_id,
      ‹name› => $o_company_details->name, ‹specialties› =>
        $o_company_details->specialties->values, ‹websiteUrl› =>
          $o_company_details->websiteUrl, ‹employeeCountRange› =>
            $o_company_details->employeeCountRange->name,
              ‹foundedYear› => $o_company_details->foundedYear,
                ‹numFollowers› =>
                  $o_company_details->numFollowers);

    // Load the view for displaying the LinkedIn company›s
    // details
    $view_params = $a_company_details;
    $this->load->view(‹linked-company›, $view_params);
    }
/*
 * This function calls the library method me to get
 * the LinkedIn company›s updates
```

```
 *
 * @param $company_id integer - Linkedin company id
 */
public function company_updates($company_id) {
  // Get the LinkedIn company›s updates
  $s_json = $this->linkedin->company_updates($company_id);
  $o_company_updates = json_decode( $s_json);

  // Processing the data received from the LinkedIn library
  $a_updates = array();
  $a_json_updates = $o_company_updates->values;
  for ($index = 0; $index < count($a_json_updates);
    $index++) {
      $o_update = $a_json_updates[$index];

      if (isset($o_update->updateContent->companyJobUpdate)) {
        $a_updates[] = array(‹type› => ‹Job Update›,
          ‹position› => $o_update->updateContent->
            companyJobUpdate->job->position->title,
              ‹url› => $o_update->updateContent->
                companyJobUpdate->job->siteJobRequest->url);
      }
    }

  // Load the view for displaying the LinkedIn
  // company›s updates
  $view_params[‹updates›] = $a_updates;
  $this->load->view(‹linked-company-updates›, $view_params);
  }
} // class closing tags
/* End of the file linkedinfo.php */
/* Location: ./application/controllers/linkedinfo.php */
```

The linkedin-me.php view file

This view file displays the LinkedIn user's details.

The following is the view code:

```
<!DOCTYPE html>
<html lang = "en">
<head>
  <meta charset = "utf-8">
  <title>My Details</title>
</head>
```

```
<body>
<table>
<tr>
  <td>Full Name:</td>
  <td><?php echo $my_details->firstName . « « .
    $my_details->lastName ; ?></td>
</tr>
<tr>
  <td>Title</td>
  <td><?php echo $my_details->headline ; ?></td>
</tr>
<tr>
  <td>My LinkedIn profile</td>
  <td><a href = «<?php echo $profile_url ?>»
    target = «_blank»>Link</a> </td>
</tr>
</table>

<div>
  <p><a href = «<?php echo site_url(<>) ; ?>»>Back to Menu</a>
    </p>
</div>
</body>
</html>
```

The view file linked-connections.php

This view file displays the LinkedIn user's connections.

The following is the view code:

```
<!DOCTYPE html>
<html lang = "en">
<head>
  <meta charset = "utf-8">
  <title>My Connections</title>
</head>
<body>
<h1>My Total connections: <?php echo $connections_count ; ?></h1>
<div>
  <p><a href = «<?php echo site_url(<>) ; ?>»>Back to Menu</a>
    </p></div>
<table>
<tr>
  <td>Picture</td>
  <td>Name</td>
```

```
    <td>Headline</td>
    <td>Industry</td>
  </tr>
    <?php foreach ($connections as $connection): ?>
  <tr>
    <td><img src = «<?php echo $connection[<picture_url>]; ?>»>
      </td>
    <td><a href = «<?php echo $connection[<url>];?>»
      target = «_blank»><?php echo $connection[<name>] ?></a></td>
    <td><?php echo $connection[<headline>]; ?></td>
    <td><?php echo $connection[<industry>]; ?></td>
  </tr>
  <?php endforeach; ?>
  </table>
  </body>
  </html>
```

The view file linked-company.php

This view file displays the LinkedIn company's details.

The following is the view code:

```
<!DOCTYPE html>
<html lang = "en">
<head>
  <meta charset = "utf-8">
  <title>Company</title>
</head>
<body>

<div>
  <p><a href = «<?php echo site_url(<>); ?>»>Back to Menu</a></p>
</div>

<table>
<tr>
  <td>Name</td>
  <td><?php echo $name; ?></td>
</tr>
<tr>
  <td>Founded</td>
  <td><?php echo $foundedYear; ?></td>
</tr>
<tr>
  <td>employeeCountRange</td>
```

```
    <td><?php echo $employeeCountRange; ?></td>
  </tr>
  <tr>
    <td>Specialties<td>
    <td>
      <ul>
        <?php foreach ($specialties as $specialty): ?>
        <li><?php echo $specialty; ?></li>
        <?php endforeach; ?>
      </ul>
    </td>
  </tr>
  <tr>
    <td>Website</td>
    <td><a href = «<?php echo $websiteUrl; ?>»>Website</a></td>
  </tr>
  <tr>
    <td>numFollowers</td>
    <td><?php echo $numFollowers; ?></td>
  </tr>
  </table>
  <div style = «margin-top: 10px;»>
    <a href = «<?php echo site_url
      (<linkedinfo/company_updates/7919>); ?>»>Updates</a>
  </div>
  </body>
  </html>
```

The view file linked-company-updates.php

This view file displays the three updates of the LinkedIn company.

The following is the view code:

```
<!DOCTYPE html>
<html lang="en">
<head>
  <meta charset = "utf-8">
    <title>Company</title>
</head>
<body>
<div>
  <p><a href = "<?php echo site_url('') ; ?>">Back to Menu</a>
    </p>
</div>
<table>
```

```php
<?php foreach ($updates as $update): ?>
<tr>
  <td>
    <ul>
      <?php foreach ($update as $key => $val): ?>
      <li><?php echo $key; ?>: <?php echo $val; ?></li>
      <?php endforeach; ?>
    </ul>
  </td>
</tr>
<?php endforeach; ?>
</table>
</body>
</html>
```

Summary

In this chapter, we have reviewed the CI libraries' scope, the different types of built-in CI echo system third-party libraries, and how to build our own libraries. We also reviewed the steps to load and use the library resources in our project. Eventually, we created several usage examples.

5
Helpers

This chapter covers the CI helpers topic, the different types of helpers, and their different usage categories, with several code examples of web applications. CI provides us with built-in helpers, enables us to integrate third-party helpers, and enables us to develop new helpers and share them with the community if we wish to. The CI helpers are powering CI efficiency and code reusability by enabling all other CI controllers using the same code instead of defining a helper function locally.

A helper file is a collection of independent procedural functions in a particular category. Each helper function performs one specific task, with no dependence on other functions. The chapter will elaborate on the CI helper's concept, definition, and usage with several examples.

The folder `system/helpers` contains the CI system's built-in helpers. The folder `application/helpers` contains all the additional helper files of CI helpers. They can be third-party helpers or created by the developer.

This chapter will primarily focus on:

- CI helpers' scope and usage
  - ° Usage categories
  - ° Using a helper
  - ° Adding a helper to the project
  - ° Loading a helper
  - ° Using helper methods
- The available CI helpers

- Examples
  - ○ Example 1: using a built-in helper
  - ○ Example 2: using third-party helpers—SSL helper
  - ○ Example 3: building our own helper—the `my_download` helper

We will begin by briefly reviewing what a helper is in a CI framework, and how we can use it for our needs across the project code resources.

CI helpers' scope and usage

The CI helper does not have access to the controller resources by default unless CI and `get_instance()` are called and used to access CI resources.

We can extend the CI helper using third-party helpers from the CI system' or we can develop our own helper.

Any application helper should be located under `application/helpers/` in the project directory.

The helper file must be in the following format:

```
application/helpers/<HELPER_NAME>_helper.php
```

For example, the SSL helper file should appear as `application/helpers/ssl_helper.php`.

The helper integration and usage within the CI project is as follows:

- Add the helper code resources to `application/helpers/myhelper_helper.php`
- Load the helper automatically or via the controller
  - ○ Automatically load a helper `myhelper` for all CI projects as follows:
    ```
    $autoload['helper'] = array('url','myhelper');
    ```
  - ○ For loading in certain specific controllers, constructors, or methods, use the following:
    ```
    $this->load->helper('myhelper');
    ```
- Use the following helper methods:
  ```
  $result = $this->myhelper->called_method($param1, aram2);
  ```

Available CI helpers

CI and the CI developers community network provide many helpers, covering a rich set of topics. We will review CI helpers as well as popular resources for third-party CI helpers.

We are also encouraged to build our own helpers, which can be used by others, and share them with the following communities:

- The `Git` community: `https://github.com`
- CI forums `http://codeigniter.com/forums/`

CI system helpers

The list of CI built-in helpers is as follows (they can be found in the `CI Directory Tree` by going to `system/helpers/`):

- Array Helper
- CAPTCHA Helper
- Cookie Helper
- Date Helper
- Directory Helper
- Download Helper
- Email Helper
- File Helper
- Form Helper
- HTML Helper
- Inflector Helper
- Language Helper
- Number Helper
- Path Helper
- Security Helper
- Smiley Helper
- String Helper
- Text Helper
- Typography Helper
- URL Helper
- XML Helper

CI third-party helpers

- ssl_helper.php

- html_manipulator_helper.php

Example 1 – using built-in helpers

In this example, we will see how to use CI build-in helpers. For this example, we will use the URL helper for generating links. The URL helper file contains functions that assist in working with URLs. We will use the URL helper function site_url(), which returns the site URL as specified in the config file.

This example will be constructed from either of the following controllers:

- application/controllers/ helperexample1.php

    This controller loads the built-in CI helper URL.

    $this->load->helper('url');

    The controller renders a view named **helper-example1-view**

- application/views/ helper-example1-view.php

    This view will use the URL helper to generate links in the view file

    Let us assume the URLs to the project root are as follows: http://mydomain. com/myproject. http://mydomain.com/myproject/helperexample1

 The source code is provided with this book via URLs.

The controller file

Now we will see how the controller loads the built-in CI URL helper so the view file will be able to use the URL helper function site_url, which generates the links.

```
class Helperexample1 extends CI_Controller {
/**
 * Index Page for this controller.
 *
 * Maps to the following URL
 *      http://example.com/index.php/welcome
 *   - or -
 *      http://example.com/index.php/welcome/index
```

```
*   - or -
* Since this controller is set as the default controller in
* config/routes.php, it's displayed at http://example.com/
*
* So any other public methods not prefixed with an underscore
*    * will
* map to /index.php/welcome/<method_name>
* @see http://codeigniter.com/user_guide/general/urls.html
*/
 public function index()
  {
         // Loading the url helper
         $this->load->helper('url');
       $this->load->view('helper-example1-view');
  }
 }
/* End of file helperexample1.php */
/* Location: ./application/controllers/helperexample1 */
```

The view file

The view file calls the URL helper function site_url. Since the controller loaded the URL helper, it's recognized by the view.

```
<!DOCTYPE html>
<html lang="en">
<head>
<meta charset="utf-8">
  <title>Menu</title>
</head>
<body>
<table>
<tr>
<td><a href="<?php echo site_url('welcome'); ?>">Welcome</a></td>
</tr>
<tr>
<td><a href="<?php echo site_url('example2/more/1/2/3');
         ?>">Example2</a></td>
</tr>
</table>
</body>
</html>
```

Example 2 – SSL helper

In this example, we will use the CI third-party SSL helper to enforce an https or HTTP URI request and response between CI and the browser. This example will be constructed from the following helpers:

- `application/helpers/ssl_helper.php`: The CI helper for SSL that implements SSL on the links.

- `application/controllers/helpersslexample.php`: This controller loads the helper and implements SSL on the links. The helper is loaded in the constructor.

  `$this->load->helper('ssl');`

- `application/views/helper-ssl-view.php`: This is the rendered view that SSL is implemented on.

Let us assume the URI to the project root is `http://mydomain.com/myproject`. `http://mydomain.com/myproject/helpersslexample`.

 The source code is provided with this book via URLs.

The helper file

This CI helper file implements the services described in the preceding section. This helper uses the built-in CI URL library and URL helper using the redirect CI URL helper function.

```php
<?php if ( ! defined('BASEPATH')) exit('No direct script access
        allowed');
if (!function_exists('force_ssl')) {
    function force_ssl()
    { // get the CI instance to access the CI resources
        $CI =& get_instance();
        // Change the base_url to have https prefix
$CI->config->config['base_url'] =
            str_replace('http://', 'https://',
            $CI->config->config['base_url']);
        if ($_SERVER['SERVER_PORT'] != 443)
        {      // redirect CI to use https URI
// so that ($CI->uri->uri_string() return
// the current URI with https prefix

            redirect($CI->uri->uri_string());
    }
```

```
        }
    }
    if (!function_exists('remove_ssl')) {
      function remove_ssl()
      {
        $CI =& get_instance();

        // Change the base_url to have http prefix
        $CI->config->config['base_url'] =
          str_replace('https://', 'http://',
          $CI->config->config['base_url']);
        if ($_SERVER['SERVER_PORT'] != 80)
        {
          // redirect CI to use http URI
          // so that ($CI->uri->uri_string() return
          // the current URI with http prefix

          redirect($CI->uri->uri_string());
        }
      }
    }
}
```

The controller file

Now we will see how the controller loads the SSL helper and calls its function
force_ssl to enforce the HTTPS URI request and response with the browser.

```
    class Helpersslexample extends CI_Controller {
      public function __construct() {
        parent::__construct();
        // Loading the ssl helper
        $this->load->helper('ssl');
        // Enforce URI request of https
        force_ssl();
      }
      /**
        * Index Page for this controller.
        *
        */
      public function index()
      {
        $this->load->helper('url');
        $this->load->view('helper-ssl-view');
      }
    }
  /* End of file helpersslexample.php */
  /* Location: ./application/controllers/helpersslexample */
```

The view file

The view file code is as follows:

```
<!DOCTYPE html>
<html lang="en">
<head>
<meta charset="utf-8">
  <title>Menu</title>
</head>
<body>
<table>
<tr>
  <td>
  <a href="<?php echo site_url('welcome'); ?>">
  Welcome - You are using https
  </a>
  </td>
</tr>
<tr>
<td><a href="<?php echo site_url('example2/more/1/2/3');
          ?>">Example2</a></td>
</tr>
</table>
</body>
</html>
```

Example 3 – building your own helper

This example uses a helper to download a very large file, of 200 MB, which can't be downloaded in one file reading.

This example will be constructed from the following helpers:

- `application/helpers/my_download_helper.php`: This is the CI helper that is used to download a very large file

- `application/controllers/classg2.php`: This is the controller that uses the `my_download` helper

- `application/views/classg2view.php`: This is the view that has a link for the file download

Let us assume that the URI to the project root is `http://mydomain.com/myproject`. Hence the URI to execute the `auth` controller for login will be `http://mydomain.com/myproject/classg2`.

The source code is provided with this book via URLs.

The helper file

This helper is used to download very large files, which can't be downloaded in one file reading. Its function, `download_large_files`, reads 1 MB in each loop until it downloads the whole file.

```php
<?php  if ( ! defined('BASEPATH')) exit('No direct script access allowed');
/**
 * CodeIgniter Download Helpers
 *
 * @package   CodeIgniter
 * @subpackage Helpers
 * @category   Helpers
 * @author Yehuda Zadik
 */
// ------------------------------------------------------------

/**
 * Download large files
 *
 * Generates headers that force a download to happen
 *
 * @access   public
 * @param       string $fullPath
 * @return      void
 */
function download_large_files($fullPath)
{
// File Exists?
if( file_exists($fullPath) )
{
  // Parse Info / Get Extension
  $fsize = filesize($fullPath);

  $path_parts = pathinfo($fullPath);
  $ext = strtolower($path_parts["extension"]);
  // Determine Content Type
  switch ($ext)
  {
    case "pdf":
      $ctype = "application/pdf";
      break;
```

```php
case "exe":
$ctype = "application/octet-stream";
 break;
case "zip":
  $ctype = "application/zip";
  break;
case "doc":
  $ctype = "application/msword";
  break;

case "xls":
  $ctyp = "application/vnd.ms-excel";
    break;
case "ppt":
  $ctype = "application/vnd.ms-powerpoint";
   break;

case "wmv":
  $ctype = "video/x-ms-wmv";
    break;
      case "gif":
  $ctype = "image/gif";
    break;
      case "png":
  $ctype = "image/png";
    break;

case "jpeg":
case "jpg":
  $ctype = "image/jpg";
        break;

default:
  $ctype = "application/force-download";
}
$file_handle = fopen($fullPath, "rb");
header('Content-Description: File Transfer');
  header("Content-Type: " . $ctype);          header('Content-
Length: ' . $fsize);

  header('Content-Disposition: attachment; filename=' .
          basename($fullPath));
while(!feof($file_handle))
{
  $buffer = fread($file_handle, 1*(1024*1024));
  echo $buffer;
```

```
        ob_flush();
        flush();     //These two flush commands seem to
have helped with performance
        }
        fclose($file_handle);
    } else
    {
        die('File Not Found');
    }
}


/* End of file my_download_helper.php */
/* Location: ./application/helpers/my_download_helper.php */
```

The controller file

The controller loads the helper my_download and calls its function, download_large_files, in order to enable the user to download large files that originally could not be downloaded, using the my_download helper.

```
<?php

class Classg2 extends CI_Controller {
    public function index()
    {
        $this->load->helper('url');
        $this->load->view('classg2view');
    }
    function download()
    {
        // Loading the helpers url, my_download
        $this->load->helper(array('url', 'my_download'));          //
FCPATH is a constant that Codeigniter sets which      // contains the
absolute path to index.php
        $fullPath = FCPATH . 'files/movie-classg2.wmv';
        // Using the helper my_download function to download      // a
very large file
        download_large_files($fullPath);
    }
}
/* End of file classg2.php */
/* Location: ./application/controllers/classg2.php */
```

The view file

The view file displays the data that contains a link for downloading the very large file.

```html
<!DOCTYPE html>
<html lang="en">
<head>
  <meta charset="utf-8">
  <title>Download large file</title>
</head>
<body>
<div id="container">
  <a href="<?php echo base_url("classg2/download")
?>">Download large file</a>
</div>
</body>
</html>
```

Summary

In this chapter we have reviewed the CI helpers, scope, the different types of built-in CI system helpers, third-party helpers, and how to build our own helpers. We also reviewed the steps to load and use helpers in our project. Finally, we saw several relevant usage examples, as follows:

- Example 1: using build-in helpers
- Example 2: using third-party helpers— SSL helper
- Example 3: building our own helper—my_download helper

6
Models

This chapter covers the CI models, their role, and their usage with several code examples of web applications. The model is responsible for handling the database it stores and retrieves database objects used by the application from a database and contains the logic implemented by the application.

Much of the data that is part of the persistent state of the application (whether that persistent state is stored in files or databases) should reside in the model objects after the data is loaded into the application. Because the model objects represent knowledge and expertise related to a specific topic, they can be reused in the application.

The model represents the application data services and can serve the application logic (commonly referred to as business logic), as well. Usually, the model is responsible for the following operations:

- **Adding, modifying, deleting, and searching the application database objects**: Generally, this includes the database operations, but implementing the same operations and invoking external web services or APIs is not unusual at all.

- **Encapsulating the application logic**: For example, the model can make data validations before storing a data object and can alert the calling application module about the problem.

The most common misuse of the CI database class is using it directly from the controller, view, or helper. A good practice is to develop the model classes to handle all the application database services.

Hence, all the other application modules can benefit, and reuse those models.

The CI models are special classes designed to handle databases or external information resources, such as Facebook (we will see an example of this in this chapter).

The CI models are the PHP classes that are designed to work with information in the database.

This chapter will primarily focus on the following topics:

- The CI model scope:
  - ° The model resource path
  - ° Loading a model
  - ° Using model methods
  - ° Connecting to a database
  - ° Business logic
- Object Relational Mapping (ORM)
- Example 1: a CRUD example
- Example 2: a business logic example
- Example 3: retrieving data from Facebook

We will begin by briefly reviewing the CI model scope and will proceed with several usage examples, covering different use cases that are combined in a real project.

Scope of the CI model

The CI model provides services for all the application modules to access the application database(s) or external information resources in an OOP fashion. Typically, the model classes will contain functions that help us retrieve, insert, and update information in the database.

This section will focus on the CI model syntax and usage guidelines, as a preface to the following usage code examples.

The model resource path

The model files are located in the folder `application/models/`, in the pattern `application/models/<MODEL_NAME>.php`.

Loading a model

Loading a model can be done automatically or via the controller. More specifically, it can be done in a certain controller's constructor or any controller's method.

- If the model is used in a few of the controller's methods, it's recommended that you load the model in those methods. The scope of the model in that case is only in those methods project and will refer to `application/models/mymodel.php`.

- If the model is used in most of the controller's methods, it's recommended that you load the model in the controller's constructor. In that case the scope of the model is in all the controller's methods project and will refer to `application/models/mymodel.php`.

```
$this->load->model('mymodel');
```

  It automatically loads a model `mymodel` for all the CI projects.

- If the model is used in most of CI's project controllers, it is recommended that you autoload it in `application/config/autoload.php`. In that case the scope of the model is in all the CI project and will refer to `application/models/mymodel.php`.

```
$autoload['model'] = array('users', 'mymodel');
```

Using model methods

Once the CI model is loaded, we will access the model functions using an object with the model name as our class. The model's method is called for performing database operations, such as retrieving, inserting, and updating data from the database.

```
// Loading the model mymodel in the controller's method
$this->load->model('mymodel');
// Calling the model's method my_function
$this->mymodel->my_function();
```

For example, let's load the model `users` and access its function `get_users`.

```
// Loading the model class
$this->load->model('usermodel');
// Calling the model to retrieve the users from the database
$view_params['users'] = $this->usermodel->get_users();
```

Connecting to a database

For more information, refer to *Chapter 2, Configurations and Naming Conventions*.

In this example, we will connect manually to a database. The following settings are done in `application/config/database.php`:

```
$config['hostname'] = '127.0.0.1';
$config['username'] = 'db_username';
$config['password'] = 'db_password';
$config['database'] = 'db_database';
$config['port'] = 'db_port';
$config['dbdriver'] = 'mysql';
```

```
$config['dbprefix']  = '';
$config['pconnect']  = TRUE;
$config['db_debug']  = TRUE;
$config['cache_on']  = FALSE;
$config['cachedir']  = '';
$config['char_set']  = 'utf8';
$config['dbcollat']  = 'utf8_general_ci';
$config['swap_pre']  = '';
$config['autoinit']  = TRUE;
$config['stricton']  = FALSE;
// Loading the database with the configuration manually
this->load->database($config);
```

Business logic

Business logic is a set of validation rules and decision criteria defined for a certain information object topic or database object.

The model can apply business logic to the database and information objects that it handles.

In the case of a social network, the model layer would take care of tasks, such as saving user data, saving friend associations, storing and retrieving user photos, finding new friends for suggestions, and so on.

Object Relational Mapping (ORM)

While CI provides the model class for the developer to expand for object-oriented database **CRUD (Create, Read, Update, and Delete)** validation, and business logic for the defined project database, there's another option that enables automatic model services. In this section, we will discuss **Object Relational Mapping (ORM)**. ORM is a new concept of converting the database scheme definition into an object-oriented database class API. It provides database CRUD services on a given database, so that the minimal code is required, instead of the full model development. More than that, the customized validation on the CRUD operation is enabled as well. Using an ORM plugin may reduce the need to self-develop our own CI models so that only special business logic activities are left to be implemented.

Today, ORM plugins provide predefined validation services, as well as user-defined services to enforce validations on CRUD requests from the application controllers, libraries, or helpers requesting the database CRUD services.

There are pros and cons of using ORM. On one hand, it simplifies a lot of the database model development for the database. On there other hand, it dictates various rules on the database scheme definition, such as defining user tables for an ORM object user, or defining the auto-increment primary key field name, such as ID, and so on.

There are several ORM plugins for CI; the most well-known and well-documented ones, with a large network of community developers, are the following:

- **Doctrine ORM** (`docs.doctrine-project.org`): This ORM plugin with the well-documented CI integration guidelines is available at `http://docs.doctrine-project.org/en/2.0.x/cookbook/integrating-with-codeigniter.html`.

- **DataMapper CodeIgniter ORM library** (`datamapper.wanwizard.eu`): It provides the CI library, such as user guide web navigator.

- Both ORM libraries provide more than just the table-based CRUD services, but can be configured to handle the cross-table relationships of the foreign key fields. They can support one-to-many, many-to-one, and many-to-many relationships, or even more complex relationships between multiple database tables.

The ORM plugins also provide validation and manipulation services on the handled database fields, such as performing trimming on a string field before it is saved to the database.

Validation services include built-in validations such as valid e-mail fields, or a field that must have the same value as another field, such as fields with an account creation password retype requirement. The full scope and usage of ORM is beyond the scope of this CI book. However, it is highly recommended that you learn more about ORM and try using the referred ORM plugins and consider using them in your CI projects.

Of course, we do provide a simple usage example of adding a record to the database, and retrieving the database records using ORM in the following section:

ORM simple operations example

For example, let's say we have a user database table with the ID as the primary key auto-increment. User name, e-mail, and password are the other fields, and if we want to add a new user record to the database, we could do so with the help of the following code:

```php
<?PHP
// We shall define the database table named users
// with ID as auto-increment, username, password, and e-mail as
// the other fields.
// ORM will create an user objet based on the users
// table scheme. We can set the variable to this object, and use
// the operational services provided by ORM for actions, such
// as save, delete, update, and add.
$u = new User();
$u->username = 'A new User';
$u->password = 'shhnew1';
$u->email = 'user@mail.com';
// To add a new user record
if ($u->save()) {
  // if saved we have a new echo 'New User Id Opened having'
  $u->id. 'User Id <br/>';
  }
else {// Show why we failed to save echo
  $u->error->string;
  }
// Getting the first three users from the database
$u = new User();
$u->limit(3)->get();
// Showing the fetched users
foreach ($u as $user_rec)
{
  echo 'User Id: '. $user_rec->id . '<br/>';
  echo 'User Name: '. $user_rec->username . '<br />';
  echo 'User Email: '. $user_rec->email. '<br/>';
  }
// Get the user with Uid = 10 if any
$u = new user();
$seek_uid = 10;

$u->where('id', $seek_uid)->get();
// Check if found
if (exist ($u)){
  echo 'User Id:'.$u->id.' Name is'.$u->username. '<br />';
  }
else echo 'No user found for user ID'. $seek_uid. '<br />';
```

This is only a very simple usage example, while ORM today provides a rich set of CRUD and validation services. Please refer to the provided links to the featured ORM plugins for more information.

Example 1 – a CRUD example

In this example, we will see how to use a CI model. For this example, we will use a model that performs these operations on the database: SELECT, INSERT, and UPDATE.

The example displays, all the products that are retrieved by the model `productmodel` at the main page in the database.

Let us assume the URI to the project root is `http://mydomain.com/myproject` and `http://mydomain.com/myproject/product`.

 The source code is provided with this book via URLs.

The main page has links for adding and editing a product. These links generate a form for editing and adding a product.

Let us assume the URI to the project root is `http://mydomain.com/myproject` and `http://mydomain.com/myproject/product/add`.

Suppose we want to edit and update the product with `product_id` 1, the link will be `http://mydomain.com/myproject/product/edit/1`. This example will be constructed from the following controller, model, and views:

- `application/controllers/product.php`: This controller loads the model product.

  ```
  $this->load->model('productmodel');
  ```

  This controller renders the following views:

  - `productsview`: This view displays all the products with links to editing and adding a product
  - `productform`: This view contains the form for adding and editing a product

- `application/models/productmodel.php`: This model contains functions that perform these operations on the database: SELECT, INSERT, and UPDATE.

- `application/views/productsview.php`: The view that displays the products.

- `application/views/productform.php`: The view that contains the form.

The controller file

The controller PHP file is located at `application/controllers/product.php`. The controller handles the product's operations, such as adding, editing, updating, and displaying the product's table.

The controller creates a form for adding and editing a product.

For more information refer to *Chapter 7, Views*.

The following are the code and inline explanations:

```php
<?php
if (!defined('BASEPATH')) exit('No direct script access allowed');
class Product extends CI_Controller {
// Accessory method for generating forms called by the methods add
// and edit.
private function load_form($form_action, $a_values = array())
{
  // Loading the form helper
  $this->load->helper('form');
  // Loading the form_validation library
  $this->load->library('form_validation');
  $view_params['form']['attributes'] = array
    ('id' => 'productform');
  $view_params['form']['action'] = $form_action;
  $product_id = isset($a_values['product_id']) ?
  $a_values['product_id']: 0;
  $view_params['form']['hidden_fields'] = array
    ('product_id' => $product_id);
  // product name details
  $view_params['form']['product_name']['label'] = array
    ('text' => 'Product name:', 'for' => 'product_name');
  $view_params['form']['product_name']['field'] = array
    ('name' => 'product_name', 'id' => 'product_name', 'value' =>
      isset($a_values['product_name']) ?
        $a_values['product_name']: '', 'maxlength' => '100',
          size' => '30', 'class' => 'input');
  // product sku details
  $view_params['form']['product_sku']['label'] = array
    ('text' => 'Product SKU:', 'for' => 'product_sku');
```

```
$view_params['form']['product_sku']['field'] = array
  ('name' => 'product_sku', 'id' => 'product_sku', 'value' =>
    isset($a_values['product_sku']) ? $a_values['product_sku']:
      '', 'maxlength' => '100', 'size' => '30',
        'class' => 'input');
// product quantity details
$view_params['form']['product_quantity']['label'] = array
  ('text' => 'Product Quantity:', 'for' => 'product_quantity');
$view_params['form']['product_quantity']['field'] = array
  ('name' => 'product_quantity', 'id' => 'product_quantity',
    'value' => isset($a_values['product_quantity']) ?
      $a_values['product_quantity']: '', 'maxlength' => '100',
        'size' => '30', 'class' => 'input');
// Form attributes validation rules
$config_form_rules = array(
  array('field' => 'product_name', 'label' => 'Product Name',
    'rules' => 'trim|required'), array('field' => 'product_sku',
      'label' => 'Product SKU', 'rules' => 'trim|required'),
        array('field' => 'product_quantity',
          'label' => 'Product Quantity',
            'rules' => 'trim|required|integer'));
$this->form_validation->set_rules($config_form_rules);
return $view_params;
}
// This controller method retrieves the products list calling the
// model productmodel's method get_products() renders the results
// in the view productsview.
public function index()
{
  // Loading the url helper
  $this->load->helper('url');

  // Manually loading the database
  $this->load->database();

  // Loading the model class
  $this->load->model('productmodel');

  // Calling the model productmodel's method get_products()to
  // retrieve the products from the database.
  $view_params['products'] = $this->productmodel->get_products();
  // Rendering the products list in the view productsview.
  $this->load->view('productsview', $view_params);
}
// This method handles the operation of adding a product to the
// database.
```

```php
public function add()
{
  // Loading the url helper
  $this->load->helper('url');

  // Manually loading the database
  $this->load->database();

  // Loading the model class
  $this->load->model('productmodel');

  $a_post_values = $this->input->post();
  $view_params = $this->load_form('product/add', $a_post_values);

  // Validating the form
  if ($this->form_validation->run() == FALSE) {
    // Validation failed
    $this->load->view('productform', $view_params);
    } else {
    $data = $a_post_values;
    array_pop($data);
    $this->productmodel->addProduct($data);

    redirect('product');
    }
  }
// This method handles the operation of editing a product
public function edit($product_id)
{
  // Loading the url helper
  $this->load->helper('url');
  // Manually loading the database
  $this->load->database();

  // Loading the model class
  $this->load->model('productmodel');

  $a_post_values = $this->input->post();
  // Checking if a form was submitted
  if ($a_post_values) {
    $a_form_values = $a_post_values;
    } else {
    // Get the values of the database
    $a_db_values = $this->productmodel->get_product($product_id);
```

```
    $a_form_values = array
      ('product_id' => $a_db_values[0]->product_id,
        'product_name' => $a_db_values[0]->product_name,
          product_sku' => $a_db_values[0]->product_sku,
            'product_quantity' => $a_db_values[0]->product_quantity);
    }

  $view_params = $this->load_form('product/edit/' . $product_id,
    $a_form_values);
  // Validating the form
  if ($this->form_validation->run() == FALSE) {
    // Validation failed
    $this->load->view('productform', $view_params);
    } else {
    $a_fields = array('product_name', 'product_sku',
      'product_quantity');
    for ($index = 0; $index < count($a_fields); $index++)
    {
      $s_field = $a_fields[$index];
      $data[$s_field] = $this->input->post($s_field)
      }
    $this->productmodel->updateProduct($product_id, $data);
    redirect('product');
    }
  }
}
}
/* End of file product.php */
/* Location: /application/controllers/product.php */
```

The model file

The model PHP file is located at `application/models/productmodel.php`.

In this example, the methods of the CI object `db` are called for generating and executing the SQL queries.

Please refer to the CI database library at `http://ellislab.com/codeigniter/user-guide/database/index.html`.

The following are the code and inline explanations:

```
<?php
class Productmodel extends CI_Model {
  // The model's constructor method
  public function __construct()
  {
```

```
  // Call the Model's parent constructor
  parent::__construct();
  }
// This method retrieves the products list and returns an array of
// objects each containing product details.
public function get_products()
{
  // Calling the CI's db object's method for generating SQL
  // queries.
  $query = $this->db->get('products');
  // returns an array of products objects
  return $query->result();
  }
// This method retrieves a specific product's details identified by
// $product_id as a parameter
public function get_product($product_id)
{
  // Calling the CI's db object's methods for generating SQL
  // queries.
  $this->db->select('*');
  $this->db->from('products');
  $this->db->where('product_id', $product_id);

  // Calling the CI's db object method for executing the query
  $query = $this->db->get();
  // Returning array of one object element containing product
  // details.
  return $query->result();
  }


// This method adds a product to the products table Parameters
// $data - The data to insert into the table
public function addProduct($data)
{
  // Calling the CI's db object method for inserting a product data
  // into the products table.
  $this->db->insert('products', $data);
  }
// This method updates a product row in the products table
// parameters $product_id - The product id, $data - The updated
// data
public function updateProduct($product_id, $data)
{
// Calling the CI's db object's methods for generating SQL queries
$this->db->where('product_id', $product_id);
```

```
    // Calling the CI's db object method for updating the product data
    // in the products table
    $this->db->update('products', $data);
    }
}
```

The view file

The view PHP file is located at application/views/productsview.php.

This view file displays a table with the products list. The following are the code and inline explanations:

```html
<!DOCTYPE html>
<html lang="en">
<head>
<meta charset="utf-8">
<title>Products List</title>
</head>
<body>
<table>
<tr>
  <td>ID</td>
  <td>Name</td>
  <td>SKU</td>
  <td>Quantity</td>
  <td>Actions</td>
</tr>

<?php foreach ($products as $product): ?>
<tr>
  <td><?php echo $product->product_id; ?></td>
  <td><?php echo $product->product_name; ?></td>
  <td><?php echo $product->product_sku ; ?></td>
  <td><?php echo $product->product_quantity ; ?></td>
  <td><a href="<?php echo site_url("product/edit/" .
    $product->product_id); ?>">Edit Product</a></td>
</tr>
<?php endforeach; ?>
</table>

<p>
  <a href="<?php echo site_url('product/add'); ?>">Add Product</a>
</p>
</body>
</html>
```

Example 2 – a business logic example

In this example, we will demonstrate business logic. Ordering a product will trigger the model to update the product's quantity and check whether it's smaller than a certain amount.

This example will be constructed from the following controllers, model, and view:

- `application/controllers/order.php`: This controller loads the model `productmodel`

- `$this->load->model(' productmodel')`: This controller renders the view `orderview`, which displays all the products, and where each product has links to ordering a product

- `application/models/productmodel.php`: This model contains functions, which retrieve products, updates its quantity, and checks its quantity

- `application/views/ orderview.php`: The view displays all the products in a table, where each row has a link for ordering the product

Let us assume the URI to the project root is `http://mydomain.com/myproject` and `http://mydomain.com/myproject/order`.

 The source code is provided with this book via URLs.

The controller file

The controller PHP file is located at `application/controllers/order.php`.

This controller is responsible for displaying the products and updates each product. If the product's quantity reaches a limit, it generates an error message.

The code and inline explanations are as follows:

```php
<?php
if (!defined('BASEPATH')) exit('No direct script access allowed');
class Order extends CI_Controller
{
  // This method retrieves the products list and returns an array
  // of objects each containing product details
  public function index()
  {
    // Loading the url helper
```

```
    $this->load->helper('url');

    // Manually loading the database
    $this->load->database();

    // Loading the model class
    $this->load->model('productmodel');

    $view_params['products'] =
      $this->productmodel->get_products();

    $this->load->view('orderview', $view_params);
    }
// This method checks the product's quantity.
// It updates the product row in the database or generates an
// error message
public function product($product_id)
{
    // Loading the url helper
    $this->load->helper('url');

    // Manually loading the database
    $this->load->database();

    // Loading the model class
    $this->load->model('productmodel');

    if (!$this->productmodel->update_quantity($product_id)) {
      mail($user_mail, 'product' . $product_id .
        "reached it's limit", 'Order product' . $product_id);
      }
    redirect('product');
  }
}
```

The model file

The model PHP file is located at `application/models/productmodel.php`.

In this example, the methods of the CI object `db` are called for generating and executing the SQL queries.

Please refer to the CI database's library available at `http://ellislab.com/codeigniter/user-guide/database/index.html`.

The code and inline explanations are as follows:

```php
<?php
class Productmodel extends CI_Model
{
  // The model's constructor method
  public function __construct()
  {
    // Call the model constructor
    parent::__construct();
    }
  // This method retrieves the products list and returns an array of
  // objects each containing product details.
  public function get_products()
  {
    // Calling the CI's db object's method for generating the
    // SQL queries.
    $query = $this->db->get('products');
    // returns an array of products objects
    return $query->result();
    }
  // This method retrieves a specific product's details
  // identified by $product_id as a parameter.
  public function get_product($product_id)
  {
  // Calling the CI's db object's methods for generating the
  // SQL queries.
  $this->db->select('*');
  $this->db->from('products');
  $this->db->where('product_id', $product_id);
  // Calling the CI's db object method for executing the query
  $query = $this->db->get();
  // Returning array of one object element containing the product
  // details.
  return $query->result();
    }
// This method adds a product to the products table parameters.
// $data - The data to insert into the table
public function addProduct($data)
{
  // Calling the CI's db object method for inserting a product data
  // into the products table.
  $this->db->insert('products', $data);
    }
// This method updates a product row in the products table
// parameters.
// $product_id - The product id
```

```
// $data - The updated data
public function updateProduct($product_id, $data)
{
  // Calling the CI's db object's methods for generating the
  // SQL queries.
  $this->db->where('product_id', $product_id);
  // Calling the CI's db object method for updating the product data
  // in the products table.
  $this->db->update('products', $data);
  }

// This method checks whether the quantity exceeds it's limit.
private function check_quantity($product_id) {
  // Calling the CI's db object's methods for generating the
  // SQL queries.
  $this->db->select('product_quantity');
  $this->db->from('products');
  $this->db->where('product_id', $product_id);
  // Calling the CI's db object method for executing the query.
  $query = $this->db->get();
  // Calling the result's method row, which returns the SQL query
  // result row.
  $row = $query->row();
  if ($row->product_quantity < 7) {
    return false;
    } else {
    return true;
    }
  }

// This method updates a product quantity and return true or false,
// if quantity reaches it's limit.
public function update_quantity($product_id)
{
  $sql = "UPDATE products SET product_quantity = product_quantity - 1
    WHERE product_id=" $product_id;

  $this->db->query($sql);

  // Checking if the quantity reached it's limit.
  if ($this->check_quantity($product_id)) {
    return true;
    } else {
    return false;
    }
  }
}
```

The view file

The PHP view file is located at `application/views/orderview.php`. This view file displays a table with the products list.

The following are the code and inline explanations:

```php
<!DOCTYPE html>
<html lang="en">
<head>
<meta charset="utf-8">
<title>Products List</title>
</head>
<body>
<table>
<tr>
  <th>ID</th>
  <th>Name</th>
  <th>SKU</th>
  <th>Quantity</th>
  <th>Actions</th>
</tr>
<?php foreach ($products as $product): ?>
<tr>
  <td><?php echo $product->product_id; ?></td>
  <td><?php echo $product->product_name;  ?></td>
  <td><?php echo $product->product_sku ; ?></td>
  <td><?php echo $product->product_quantity ; ?></td>
  <td><a href="<?php echo site_url("order/product/" .
    $product->product_id); ?>">Order Product</a></td>
</tr>
<?php endforeach; ?>
</table>
</body>
</html>
```

Example 3 – retrieving data from Facebook

In this example, we will use the CI built-in model to retrieve data from Facebook.

The example displays a Facebook user name and picture and displays the user's Facebook friends.

This example uses Facebook PHP SDK as a CI library. It can be downloaded from `https://github.com/facebook/php-sdk`. For more information, refer to *Chapter 4, Libraries*.

This example will be constructed from the following controllers, model, and view:

- `application/controllers/fbpage.php`: This controller loads the model `fbmodel`
- `$this->load->model('fbmodel')`: This controller renders the view `fbview`, which displays the user's Facebook picture and name, and table, which contains the user's friends' names and links to their profiles
- `application/models/fbmodel.php`: This model contains functions that retrieve data from Facebook
- `application/views/fbview.php`: This view displays Facebook data

Let us assume the URI to the project root is `http://mydomain.com/myproject` and `http://mydomain.com/myproject/fbpage`.

 The source code is provided with this book via URLs.

The controller file

The controller PHP file is located at `application/controllers/fbpage.php`.

The controller is responsible for getting the access token from Facebook and redirecting the Facebook user to the Facebook login page to confirm the Facebook app's permission.

The controller is also responsible for getting the Facebook user's details and friends via the model and rendering the view page accordingly.

For more information about Facebook API usage and development, please refer to the Facebook developer page available at `http://developers.facebook.com/`.

The following are the code and inline explanations:

```php
<?php
class Fbpage extends CI_Controller {
  public function __construct() {
    parent::__construct();
    // Extremely important!!!
```

```
  // Due to the fact that the CI handles classes for
  // $_GET, $_POST, and $_COOKIE parse_str is called to
  // copy the variables sent by Facebook to the $_REQUEST var,
  // so that the Facebook SDK can do its checks.
  // This is done in order to avoid infinite redirect loop.
  parse_str($_SERVER['QUERY_STRING'], $_REQUEST);
  }
// This method retrieves Facebook data of a Facebook user and
// displays personal details and some of his  friends.
// It checks if a Facebook token is valid, if it's valid,
// then it displays his details, otherwise it produces
// the token.
public function index() {
  $a_config = array('appId' => $fb_API, 'secret'=> $fb_secret,
    'cookie' => true);
  $this->load->library('facebook', $a_config);
  // Checking if the user is logged in and confirms
  // the app's permissions.
  if ($user = $this->facebook->getUser()) {
    // Get the Facebook token
    $access_token = $this->facebook->getAccessToken();
    // Loading the fbmodel
    $this->load->model('fbmodel');
    // Updating the token
    $this->fbmodel->set_token($access_token);
    // Get a Facebook user's profile details
    $user_profile = $this->fbmodel->get_user_profile();
    // Getting the Facebook user ID
    $uid = $user_profile['id'];

    // Retrieving a Facebook user's details
    $me = $this->fbmodel->get_me_by_fql($uid);
    // Get a Facebook user's friends
    $friends = $this->fbmodel->get_friends();
    $view_params = array('me' => $me, 'friends' => $friends);
    // Loading the view
    $this->load->view("fbview", $view_params);
    } else {
    // The Facebook parameters for the Facebook login URL,
    // where scope consists the Facebook app's permissions.
    $a_params = array ('fbconnect' => 0,
      'scope' => offline_access, publish_stream',
        'cookie' => true);
    // The Facebook login URL page
    $login_url= $this->facebook->getLoginUrl($a_params);
```

```php
    // Redirecting the Facebook user to the login URL.
    // After the Facebook user confirms the permissions
    // required by the app; he is redirected back to the
    // index page.
    header('Location:'. $login_url);
    }
  }
}
```

The model file

The model PHP file is located at `application/models/fbmodel.php`.

The model is responsible for interacting with the Facebook SDK and retrieving the Facebook user's details and friend lists. The model uses the Facebook FQL mechanism.

For more information about Facebook API usage and development, please refer to the Facebook developer page available at `http://developers.facebook.com/`.

The code and inline explanations are as follows:

```php
<?php
class fbmodel extends CI_Model {
  // The Facebook app's token
  private $token;
  public function __construct() {
    // Call the model constructor
    parent::__construct();
  }

  // This method sets the model class's private token value
  public function set_token($token) {
    $this->token = $token;
  }

  // This method returns an array, which contains the Facebook user
  // profile.
  public function get_user_profile() {
    // Getting the CI main class to get access to the Facebook
    // library.
    $ci =& get_instance();

    // Getting the Facebook user's profile
    $user_profile = $ci->facebook->api('/me');
```

```
            return $user_profile;
        }

        // This method returns an array, which contains a Facebook user's
        // details.
        public function get_me_by_fql($uid) {
            // Getting the CI main class to get access to the Facebook
            // library.
            $ci =& get_instance();
            // The SQL query to send to Facebook $fql = SELECT uid, name,
            // pic_big FROM user WHERE uid=" $uid;
            $param = array('method' => 'fql.query', 'query' => $fql,
                'callback' => '');

            // Getting the Facebook user's details
            $fqlResult = $ci->facebook->api($param);
            // Returning an array, which contains the required details
            return $fqlResult;
        }

        // This method returns an array of a Facebook user's friend.
        public function get_friends() {
            // Getting the CI main class to get access to the Facebook
            // library
            $ci =& get_instance();
            // Getting the Facebook user's friends
            $friends = $ci->facebook->api('/me/friends');

            // Returning an array, which contains a Facebook user's friend
            return $friends;
        }
    }
```

The view file

The view PHP file is located at `application/views/fbview.php`.

This view file displays a Facebook user's details and a table with their friend details.

The code and inline explanations are as follows:

```
<!DOCTYPE html>
<html lang="en">
<head>
  <meta charset="utf-8">
```

```html
    <title>My facebook details</title>
</head>
<body>

<div id="my_details">
  <div id="picture"><img src="<?=$me[0]['pic_big'] ?>"></div>
  <div id="my_name"><?=$me[0]['name'] ?></div>
</div>
<table>
<tr>
  <th>Name</th>
  <th>Link to friend</th>
</tr>
<?php foreach ($friends['data'] as $friend): ?>
<tr>
  <td><?=$friend['name']?></td>
  <td><a href='http://www.facebook.com/<?=$friend["id"]?>'>To
    friend</a></td>
</tr>
<?php endforeach; ?>
</table>
</body>
</html>
```

Summary

In this chapter, we have reviewed the CI model scope, business logic, and ORM. We have made the following examples in this chapter:

- Example 1: a CRUD example
- Example 2: a business logic example
- Example 3: retrieving data from Facebook

7
Views

This chapter covers the process flow to render views, the process flow within the view file, different type of views, and their role and usage with several code examples of web applications.

The views are programmatic portions that provide content to the browser to be executed on the client side (that is, the user PC) to make the user-interface session on the local computer.

The PHP view file rendered output returns from the server as an HTTP response content to the requesting browser application (that is, requesting via submitting a URI in the browser navigation area).

Initially, the browser sends a URI request that the user types in, to a default or specific controller method, such as `http://mysite.com/myapp/helloworld`.

The called controller method processes the request, performs its decision making, and may use the other CI resources, such as helpers, libraries, models, and eventually renders a view back as an HTTP response to the browser HTTP request that initiates the controller operation. The HTML file returned to the browser includes HTML, CSS, and JavaScript. The browser executes the received rendered view from the server, and uses it to perform the user-interface session (visual elements, and UI elements, such as buttons, scrollbars, and navigation elements); we see and operate via the browser to navigate to other page views or get specific information or media by issuing a page anchor, button, clicking on the icon, and so on. The described action causes another HTTP request(s), either synchronous (mostly anchor) or asynchronous AJAX request(s) handled by JavaScript embedded in the web page.

The CI view is a PHP file that may contain part or all of the following: PHP statements, HTML tags, CSS, JavaScript program, Flash, images, and media sources. In CI, a view file may contain the PHP code that uses the controller-provided parameters, or even call the CI helpers, libraries, or model directly to generate the output that is part of the generated HTML file response. The generated PHP output can be strings or numeric values incorporated in the HTML tags, or even a whole HTML page.

This chapter will primarily focus on the following topics:

- The CI view scope:
    - The CI view resources path
    - The rendering flow
    - Client-side flexibility
    - Accessing libraries/helpers within a view
    - Forms
    - Using AJAX
    - View parser configuration issues
    - Integrating jQuery or other client-side libraries
- View rendering plugins (view template plugin example)
- Example 1: HTML5 location powered by Google Maps
- Example 2: user feedback powered by AJAX and the jQuery UI

We will begin by briefly reviewing the CI view scope, and will proceed with several usage examples covering different use cases that can be combined in a real project.

Scope of the CI view

The CI view is enabled with great flexibility to integrate the client-side third-party resources, as well as accessing the CI resources of the CI libraries, helpers, and models.

This section will focus on the CI view syntax and usage guidelines, as a preface to the coming usage code examples.

We can extend the CI library using the third-party libraries from the CI echo system or develop our own libraries.

The CI view resources path

In a CI project, the view files are located under the `application/views/` directory or any subdirectory to this path. For example, we can build under `application/views/` subdirectories, for let's say, two different view categories to improve the clarity of the file structure in our project. The following screenshot shows the views location in a CI project directory tree:

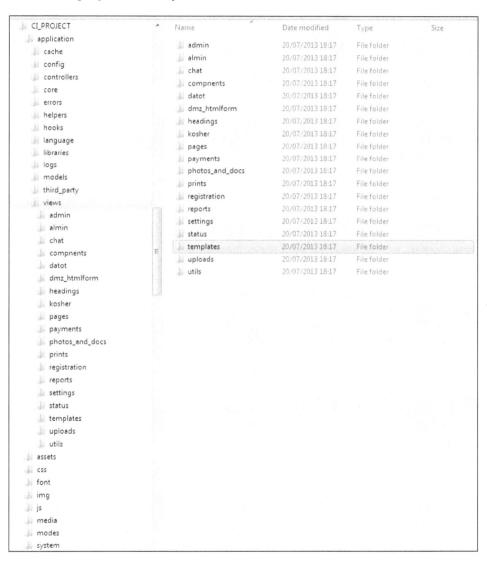

For example, to render a template file located at `Application/views/templates/` named `home.php`, we shall write the following code:

```
$this->load->view('templates/home');
//The following load view call, render a view using all its optional
parameters
$this->load->view('view_file', // PHP view file to render
$view_params,  // parameters array for view
FALSE  //  FALSE - default. to output
//   TRUE - back as string
  );
```

In this example, `view_file` is referring to the CI resource PHP view file `application/views/view_file.php`.

`$view_params` is the array of parameters (scalar/array in each entry) for the view file, as we have demonstrated at several places earlier, so that each array key, let's say, `name`, becomes the `$name` PHP variable in the view to use.

In case we wish to get the processed view into a buffer, for, special processing, caching, or any other processing purpose, for example you may call the following example:

```
$view_buffer=$this->load->view
('sectionA/view_file', $params, TRUE);
```

Note that the third parameter's value is set to `TRUE` (the default value is set to `FALSE`, and echoes the view to the standard output; in the case of the controller rendering, this means it will be returned as an HTTP response to the browser, issuing the request from the controller).

The preceding example refers to the following view file: `application/views/sectionA/view_file.php`.

The rendering flow

The view is rendered by the controller. The controller provides the parameters to the rendered PHP view file to use them.

The controller uses the following built-in CI load library: `$this->load->view('my_view',$data);`

Otherwise, the controller uses the third-party rendering service library. In this chapter we will use such a library. The CI controller rendering is done by the CI load view library, and that optionally accepts the `$data` of parameters and objects that the rendered PHP view file can use. See the following code for example:

```
$data['myval'] = 'Hello';
$this->load->view('my_view',$data);
```

The rendered PHP view file `application/views/my_view.php` uses the `$data` parameters provided via the load library as follows:

```
<H1><?PHP echo $myval; ?></H1>
```

Note that the controller defines the data as follows:

```
$data['myval'] = 'Hello';
```

While the usage at the PHP view file rendered will be as follows:

```
<H1><?PHP echo $myval; ?></H1>
```

Later, the PHP view file will be executed, so that the HTML generated code will be as follows:

```
<H1>Hello</H1>
```

The entire PHP view file that is rendered, including the PHP executions, will generate the view HTML file that will be returned to the browser via HTTP to be executed locally.

View flexibility

CI provides the flexibility for the PHP view file code to use any client-side JavaScript/CSS/HTML, or other JavaScript libraries in the view files, without any requirement to declare them at the server-side controller, as it occurs in some other platforms.

Furthermore, the CI view can access any other CI resources, such as the CI libraries, the CI models, or the CI helpers, as if it were the rendering controller of the view; for example, accessing a session parameter directly.

```
$param = $this->session->userdata('param1' );
```

Also, the CI view can call a CI library method directly in the same fashion as the rendering controller does (assuming the rendering controller loads this library).

```
$calc = $this->my_lib->my_lib_calc( $param);
<H1><?PHP echo $calc; ?></H1>
```

Accessing the libraries/helpers

As mentioned earlier, the CI PHP view file can access any of the CI resources, such as calling the CI helpers, libraries, or models in the same way the controller does.

The following is a more elaborated and complete example of a PHP CI view file, accessing CI resources, such as libraries/models/helpers:

```
<HTML>
<?PHP
// URI is a built-in CI library
// if the rendering controller for this view was
// http://mysite/myproject/mycontroller/test3
// the segment(1) = mycontroller - the controller name
// the segment(2) = test3 - the controller method
$the_controller = $this->uri->segment(1);
$the_method = $this->uri->segment(2);
?>
<H1>This View Rendered by Controller
<?=$the_controller; ?> </H1>
<H1>Using its method named <?=$the_method; ?></H1>
```

Forms

The CI PHP view file can contain any number of HTML data entry forms to accept the input data from the browsing user. We can use the CI form helper service to simplify the data entry buildup powered validation services.

The CI form helper provides a useful and comprehensive set of PHP functions for many data entry and input fashions. Among them we can find the data entry of the text field, the area text field, the radio button, checkbox, combo box, and menu option.

The following is a list of the most common CI form helper functions:

- `form_open()`
- `form_input()`
- `form_dropdown()`

- `form_password()`
- `form_upload()`
- `form_textarea()`
- `form_multiselect()`
- `form_checkbox()`
- `form_radio()`
- `form_close()`

The CI form helper generates an HTML portion that is rendered as part of the HTML file that is returned to the browser.

For example, let's take a look at a drop-down selection example of a color pickup.

```
<HTML>
<?PHP
$attr = ' class="nice_field" ';
$options = array();
$options[0] = 'Blue';
$options[1] = 'Green';
$options[2] = 'Yellow';
$default    = 1;
echo form_dropdown("color", $options, $default, $attr);
?>
```

The `form_dropdown` helper will generate the following code:

```
<select class="nice_field" name="color">
<option value="0">Blue</option>
<option selected=»selected» value=»1»>Green</option>
<option value=»2»>Yellow</option>
</select>
```

For more information, refer to the CI form help user manual.

AJAX

Asynchronous JavaScript and XML services (AJAX) (http://en.wikipedia.org/wiki/Ajax) of JavaScript/jQuery integration within a view is critical today in almost any web application. It provides an advanced user experience by operating asynchronously in parallel to the user operations, and updates only certain HTML selector portions and not the entire page as anon AJAX updates operate.

AJAX has many use case examples to enhance the user experience. The following are few common usage examples:

- Autocomplete while the user typing into a field all the matches found shown in a pop-up list for the user to choose. Without AJAX autocomplete the UI service is almost impossible.

- When submitting a form data entry using AJAX enables to issue the server submission to store or process the date and show the result only in a specific selector (notification massage), instead of refreshing the whole page as form with the action, submission requires. (Format: Bullet)

- When browsing many information pages (called pagination) and clicking on a certain page number to view. AJAX enables rendering the selected page to view within a selection DIV in the whole HTML page without refreshing the whole page. (Format: Bullet End)

Currently, AJAX is becoming an essential view component, mostly enabled via the popular jQuery library, which makes it easy to use. AJAX is an extremely valuable UI asset for building smart and interactive views. For example, the following is an example of the AJAX service that, for a given **SSN (Social Security Number)**, provides the person's name and phone number in the defined selectors, if found, or alerts, if else. Whenever the user is clicking on the **Get Info** button, an AJAX call is triggered, and an asynchronous AJAX call to an AJAX controller is sent with the SSN to get the person's record. When the response is returned, if the SSN was found, the phone and name of the person will be updated. Otherwise, a notification will be provided that the SSN person's record was not found.

The following is the code implementing the process described previously, where the AJAX call is the heart of the operation:

```
<script type="text/javascript">
function get_person_info
  (SSN_val, name_sel, phone_sel, err_sel) {
  /*
  //SSN_val -the value of the SSN user typed in to search
  //name_sel-the name input that the Ajax will update if SSN found
..//phone_sel-the phone selector to be update if SSN found as well
  //err_sel-the error message area, to explain error such as SSN
  //not found or some other error occurred.
  */
  varajax_url = '<?php echo base_url();?>ajax/get_person_info';
  $.ajax({
    type: "POST",      //Very important POST is the best
    url: ajax_url,
    // the URI of the AJAX server side controller method that will
```

```
processes this request
    data: {SSN: SSN_val},
    // SSN is the parameter name
    // SSN_val is the value
    dataType: "json",
    //the retuned data expected to be JSON
    success: function(data) {
      // the data is the array conversion of the JSON data
      // retuned to ease our usage in the JavaScript!
      if(data.result=='found') {
        // Let's show the name and phone of the person with the
        //given SSN
        $(name_sel).val(data.name);
        $(phone_sel).val(data.phone);
      } else{
        // SSN Not found in the database!
        // Let's notify SSN has no person match
        $(err_sel).css ('color', 'red');
        $(err_sel).text('No person found with SSN' + SSN_val );
      }
    },
    error : //Ajax error occurred such as Ajax server not found
    //and so on
    function ( msg ) { alert ('Error:' + msg )
    $(err_sel).css ('color', 'red');
    $(err_sel).text ('Error:' + msg);
  }
});
// Wait for the document to be ready and bind the user click
// on the #get id selector to call the AJAX search service
// with the user typed SSN
$(function(){
  $('#get').click( function(){
    get_person_info ($('#SSN').val(),
    '#name',
    '#Phone',
    '#err_sel'
  );
  });
});
</script>
```

The following is the portion of the HTML form itself:

```
<form>
<label>Enter SSN</label>
<input type='text' name="SSN" id="SSN">
<button id='get'>Get Info</button>
<BR/>
<label>Name</label><B id='name'></B><BR/>
<label>phone</label><B id='phone'></B>
</form>
<B id='err_sel'></B>
```

Parser configuration issues

The view is parsed by the CI parser before it is rendered back to the requesting browser. The default syntax to echo a PHP parameter / calculated expression value within the HTML tags is `<?PHP echo trim($param); ?>`.

However, CI provides automatic PHP short tag parsing support configuration at `application/config/config.php` and at the configuration parameter `$config['rewrite_short_tags'] = TRUE;`.

If `rewrite_short_tags` is set to TRUE, we can use the short tag of `<?=trim($param)?>`.

An important note on this is that in terms of debugging, the non-short/regular PHP echo format is preferred, as the short form errors might be more difficult to trace in this fashion. However, since this fashion is used in many code projects we've seen, we are mentioning it as well.

Integrating jQuery or other client-side libraries

CI provides the freedom to integrate any client-side libraries, so that CI does not have to be specially configured to, or we do not need to perform any special CI declarations.

The client-side integration is performed in the same fashion, as if no platform is being used; they are completely transparent. However, CI provides client-side jQuery code generation services via PHP, such as building the JavaScript library to create jQuery code, as part of the controller coding.

```
$this->load->library('javascript');
```

However, for the latest jQuery and many other JavaScript-based solutions today, there's no need to use this fashion of rendered JavaScript portions, but we can use the JavaScript A-Z in the view itself instead. A great resource for the (wow level) JavaScript libraries can be found in the largest resource for the JavaScript libraries we've found so far at `http://www.jsdb.io`.

Many more cool links for client-side platforms can be found at `https://delicious.com/eliorr1961`.

Note that the directory path for the sources in the CI views is calculated, as if the view file is in the project root.

For example, let's say the JavaScript library is located at `<Project_root>/javascript/myjs.js`.

And the view is located either at the `<Project_root>/application/views/view1.php` or `<Project_root>/application/views/topicB/view2.php` view path under `views`.

After we provide the root path via the base tag using the built-in CI URL helper `<base href="<?php echo base_url() ?>"/>`, both will load `myjs.js` as follows:

```
<script type='text/javascript'src="javascript/myjs.js" ></script>
```

They load as if they were located at the project root. This is due to the fact that CI processes the requests and rendering views as part of the root directory `index.php`. Hence, all the directory paths for SRC or INCLUDE from view PHP portions are considered, as if they occurred from the project root directory. This is due to the fact that all URIs to the project are executed by `index.php`. So for all the project code, the directory path is as though your code was in the same directory of `index.php` or at the CI project root directory.

Plugins for rendering view

As mentioned at the beginning of this chapter, we can use third-party libraries to enable us to create more advanced rendering services in a template layout fashion.

For example, the CodeIgniter template class by *Colin Williams* available at `http://www.williamsconcepts.com/ci/libraries/template/index.html`.

This plugin enables us to define the rendered page as a **Lego** fashioned layout with predefined page regions, so that we can have a different PHP CI view to render each of them.

This way we can have great reusability and a unified look, and fill in the entire application page, which in many cases is a good **UX (User Experience)** practice. In this case, the user, let's say, will know that on the top they will have a certain main navigation area, on the right certain status info and operational shortcuts, and so on.

We can define one or more layouts, so that each page layout template will have its region's organization. Each region is commonly defined within a DIV.

Having several template layouts, we can initially choose the proper layout we want to use, and then we will load its region content using the CI views defined for each region. For example, let's say we want to have a certain layout named `default`.

The `default` template's main layout will be named, `template`, for example, using the view file `main_template.php`, so that `main_template.php` will include the following regions:

- `header`
- `upper_navigation`
- `content`
- `footer`

We shall perform the following configurations at `application/config/template.php`.

 This is not the CI built-in plugin, but an additional plugin with the library and configuration file, and other assets we have installed to our CI project.

```
//The default template shall be defined as follow:
//Note, more templates can be defined in the same fashion
$template['default']['template'] = 'main_template';
$template['default']['regions'] = array
  ('header', 'upper_navigation', 'content', 'footer');
```

The `main_template` refers to `application/views/main_template.php`.

The content of `main_template.php` will include rendering of all the defined template regions as follows:

```
<html>
<body>
<div><?=$header;?></div>
<div ><?= $upper_navigation;?></div>
<div><!--main content area -->
<?= $content; ?>
</div>
```

```
<!-- #footer -->
<?=$footer;?>
</body>
</html>
```

In order to use the preceding template plugin, we will do the following:

First, load the template library in the CI controller constructor/s where we want to use the template. Remember that the template library is located at <Project_root>/application/libraries/Template.php.

We shall load the template library as follows:

```
$this->load->library('template');
```

```
<Project_root>/application/libraries/Template.php
```

```
    $this->load->library('template');
```

Then, we will load the specific template file we have configured (we can define many to choose from), let's say, in the controller constructor, we will also assume that all the controller methods use the same template.

```
//set the selected template from the template config we want
//to use
$this->template->set_template('default');
```

Now, for rendering the template regions into a rendered view using the predefined view . We will do as follows:

For each template region at, let's say, <Project_root>/application/views/, we shall load it to the corresponding region as follows:

```
$this->template->write_view ('header', 'header_view', $data);.
$this->template->write_view
('upper_navigation', 'upper_navigation_view', $data );
$this->template->write_view ('content', 'content_view', $data);
$this->template->write_view ('footer', 'footer_view', $data);
```

Now the template regions are rendered with their region view files. We can render the whole template with all its regions as follows:

```
// Now, we have all the regions rendered into the
// template instance buffer, we can render them all to
// the desired template base page.
$this->template->render();
```

The point to remember is that templates have great pros, but also some cons. The template dictates a very strict way of rendering a template base page that does not always have the desired flexibility, so that we may find ourselves writing several templates and switch between them, according to the UI situation.

Example 1 – HTML5 location powered by Google Maps

In this example, we will expand the Google Maps integration example from *Chapter 4, Libraries,* so that there will be a new option of showing the user where they are located on the Google Map. For doing so, we will use the HTML5 `navigator. geolocation` service to request the browsing user to share its location with the application. If the user agrees, and is using an advanced browser, such as the latest Firefox, Chrome builds that support to this service. Once we get the values, we will collect the geolocation, and call a controller method to prepare the Google Map of that area to render a Google Map view with the option `navigator`. We will use the HTML5 `navigator.geolocation` service as follows:

```
navigator.geolocation.getCurrentPosition(getLocation,
locationFail);
```

Here, `getLocation` is called, if the location was successfully fetched, and `locationFail`, if it was failed.

We will start with the controller first.

The controller file

The controller PHP file is located at `application/controllers/gmaps.php`. The following is the controller code based on *Chapter 4, Libraries,* for the extended Google Maps API integration example, where the new parts of code are highlighted:

```
class Gmaps extends CI_Controller
{
// Extends the CI controller to be our Gmaps controller powered by
// the Google API wrapper library.
  // Setting the initialization parameters of Google Maps
  // Library Mapper for the window size where the
  // user interaction with Google Maps created window will occur
private $user_lon = 0;
private $user_lat = 0;
function __construct()
{parent::__construct();
```

```
        $this->load->library('googlemaps');
        // Set the map window sizes:
        $config['map_width'] = "1000px";  // map window width
        $config['map_height'] = "1000px";  // map window height
        $this->googlemaps->initialize($config);
    }
    function index()
    {
    /*Initialize and setup Google Maps for our App starting with
    3 marked places: London, UK, Bombai, India, Rehovot, Israel
    */
    // Initialize our map for this use case of show 3 places
    // altogether.
    // let the zoom be automatically decided by Google for
    // showing the several places in one view
    $config['zoom'] = "auto";
    $this->googlemaps->initialize($config);
    //Define the places we want to see marked on Google Map!
    $this->add_visual_flag ('London, UK');
    $this->add_visual_flag ('Bombai, India');
    $this->add_visual_flag ('Rehovot, Israel');

    // **NEW CODE **
    // optional user location if user allow it and was fetched
    // successfully
    if ( $this->is_user_location_defined () ) {
      $this->add_visual_flag ($this->get_user_location ());
    }

    $data = $this->load_map_setting ();
    // Load our view, passing the map data that has just been
    //created.
    $this->load->view('google_map_view', $data);
}
// ** NEW CODE **
function user_location ($lat=0, $lon=0)
{
  // This is a new code we add for showing the
  //Geolocation fetched from the view base HTML5 Geolocation
  //service.
  //Initialize our map with it if it is set.
  if (! $lat&& ! $lon ) $this->index();

  // They are ok - let's keep them
  $this->user_lat = $lat;
```

```
    $this->user_lon = $lon;
    $config['center'] = $this->get_user_location ();
    // Define the address we want to be on the map center
    $config['zoom'] = "5";
    // since its approximate location is country level
    $this->googlemaps->initialize($config);
    //Add visual flag
    $this->add_visual_flag ($config['center']);
    $data = $this->load_map_setting ();
    // Load our view, passing the map data that has just been
    //created.
    $this->load->view('google_map_view', $data);
    }
// ** NEW CODE
functionis_user_location_defined ( ) {
    return ( $this->user_lat != 0 ) || ( $this->user_lon!= 0 );
    }
// ** NEW CODE
functionget_user_location ( ) {
    return $this->user_lat.", ".$this->user_lon;
    }

functionlondon()
{
  // as before
  }

functionbombai()
{
  // as before
  }
functionrehovot()
{
  // as before
  }
functionload_map_setting ( ) {
  // as before
  }
functionadd_visual_flag ( $place ) {
  // as before
  }
}
//End class Gmaps
```

The view file

The view PHP file is located at `application/views/google_map_view.php`. The following is the view file code based on *Chapter 4*, *Libraries*, for the extended Google Maps API usage example view, where the new parts of code are highlighted.

Here, we add an HTML5 service in JavaScript to collect the user's geolocation, and call the controller method `user_location ($lat=0, $lon=0)`.

```
<!DOCTYPE html">
<meta http-equiv="Content-type" content="text/html;
  charset=utf-8" />
<html>
<head>
<script src="http://code.jquery.com/jquery-latest.js"
  type ='text/javascript'></script>
<script>
// New Code to get the user Geolocation and ask the controller to
// render a Google Map for it.
var latitude = 0;
var longitude = 0;
functionshow_on_map () {
  var DIRECTORY_SEPARATOR = '/';

  // Prepare the URL path of calling the Gmaps controller method
  // user_location with latitude and longitude coordinates as
  // parameters using the CI naming convention of
  // ControllerName/methodName/Param1/Param2
  Var url_to_show =
  '<?php echo base_url(); ?>index.php/gmaps/user_location/' +
  longitude + DIRECTORY_SEPARATOR + latitude;
  // Use jQuery to issue the HTTP controller call and rendering
  // request
  $(location).attr('href', url_to_show );
  }
$(document).ready(function() {
  // if user clicks on the <li> for getting its Geolocation
  $('#getmylocation').click(checkLocation);
  functioncheckLocation() {
    // Check if the browser supports the HTML5 Geolocation
    // Note that navigator.geolocation will pop a request from
    // the user to allow getting its location (Privacy)
    if (navigator.geolocation) {
      // It does so let the user be notified
      $('#notifications').html
        ( 'fetching your location, wait...' );
```

```
      $('#notifications').css ( 'color', 'blue' );

      // Try to fetch the latitude/longitude of the browsing user
      //and provides the callbacks
      // Success: getLocation
      // Failure: locationFail
      navigator.geolocation.getCurrentPosition
        (getLocation, locationFail);
    }

else {
    $('#notifications').html
      ( 'Sorry, your browser settings does not enable fetching your
        Geolocation');
    } // ends checkLocation()
    //this is what happens if getCurrentPosition is successful
    functiongetLocation(position) {
      latitude = position.coords.latitude;
      longitude = position.coords.longitude;
      // Notify user for its location:
      $('#notifications').html
      ( 'Your approx. position :
        (' + latitude + ',' + longitude + ')' );
      $('#notifications').css ( 'color', 'green' );
      // Two seconds after the notification to user we have the
      // location issue call to the controller to show it on
      // the Google Map
      setTimeout ( show_on_map, 2000);
      }
    //this is what happens if getCurrentPosition is unsuccessful
    //(getCurrentPositionerrorCallback)
    functionlocationFail() {
      $('#notifications').html
        ('Sorry, your browser could not fetch your location ...');
      $('#notifications').css ('color', 'red');
      }
});
</script>
<!—As Before..  -->
<!—Notification selector  -->
<HR></HR>
<DIV style='background:lightgreen;width:300px;'>
<span id='notifications'>...</span>
</DIV>
<HR></HR>
```

```
<ul>
<!-- Let the User Always Get Back to the default Zoom out with
   all places marked>
<li><?php echo anchor
   ("index.php/gmaps", '<B>See All Locations</B>' ) ?></li>
<!—If user clicks this one the Geo Location service will start -->
<li id = 'getmylocation' style = 'cursor: pointer;
   color: blue; decoration: underline'> Show Me My Location</li>
<!—As Before..  -->
```

Example 2 – user feedback powered by AJAX and the jQuery UI

In this example, we will show how we can use the jQuery UI with AJAX to call a CI AJAX controller method to collect the user feedback, and submit it without refreshing/rendering a page.

We will reuse and expand the login example from *Chapter 3, Usage and Scope of Controllers,* so if a user is logged in, we will log the feedback with the user ID kept in the session, while if not, we will log it as anonymous user feedback.

Remember the following things:

- **Username**: reg_user,
- **Password**: 111111111 (9 by 1s) for regular user login

The reused and extended resources are as follows:

- auth.php: No change here
- ajax_handler.php: This is the new AJAX handler controller
- users_model.php: This is the extended user model
- logged_in_view.php: This is the extended view for regular user login

We expand the code to include the new Ajax_handler to keep the jQuery UI dialog submission of the browsing user feedback, as well as get the user logged message via the AJAX asynchronous interface. Note that we check in Ajax_handler to see whether the request is AJAX or not. And if it's not, we issue the following URL in the browser:

http://photographersnav.com/ci_utils/index.php/ajax_handler.

We will get a notification in the browser that this is a bad request.

The `users_model` resource is expanded to provide a few more services, which are as follows:

- `get_logged_in_user()`: This function is used to return the logged in user record if logged in or NULL otherwise. `get_user_rec ( $uid )` to get a specific user record based on his/her ID.

- `keep_user_feedback ($feedback)`: This function is used to keep the user feedback in the database with its user ID, if logged in.

- `get_user_feedbacks ($uid)`: This function get all the user feedback messages save till now in the database as an array of the database objects. Each feedback database row returned have the feedback message and its timestamp formatted as HTML and returned via the JSON format back to the AJAX caller to be shown to the end user via the jQuery selector based HTML rendering (for example, `$(selector).html (The_html_item_returned_from_server)`).

The `logged_in_view` resource is expanded to provide the user with the new services as follows:

- Add a new feedback button, which when clicked pops-up a jQuery UI dialog for this purpose

- Show the feedback log button, which when clicked shows a scrollable list of the user feedback

Now let us review the source code itself.

The ajax_handler.php controller file

The controller PHP file is located at `application/controllers/ajax_handler.php`. The code and inline explanations are as follows:

```
<?php if (!defined('BASEPATH'))
  exit('No direct script access allowed');
class Ajax_handler extends CI_Controller {
  function __construct()
  {parent::__construct();
    /* Standard libraries, database & helper URL loaded via the
      auto load
    */
    if (!$this->input->is_ajax_request())
    {exit( "Bad Request ignored! - Your info has been logged for
      further investigation of attacking the site!");
    }
  /* ------ Our Users Model ---------- */
```

```
    $this->load->model ( 'users_model' );
}

functionsave_user_feedback () {
    // Get the feedback content
    $feedback = $this->input->post('feedback');
    // Get if the user is logged in keep the user id
    $this->users_model->keep_user_feedback($feedback);
    }
functionget_user_feedback_log () {
    $user = $this->users_model->get_logged_in_user ();
    if ( $user ) $uid = $user->id;
    $user_feedback_rows =
        $this->users_model->get_user_feedbacks( $uid );
    $html = '';
    foreach ($user_feedback_rows as $row )
    $html.= $row->timestamp.' -  <B>'.$row->feedback.'</B><BR/>';
    $result = array ('result' => $html);
    echojson_encode ($result);
    return;
    }
} // End Ajax_handler
```

The users_model.php model file

The model PHP file is located at application/models/users_model.php.
The code and inline explanations are as follows:

```
<?php if (!defined('BASEPATH'))
exit('No direct script access allowed');
class Users_model extends CI_Model {
    function __construct()
    {parent::__construct();
    }
    functioncheck_login ($user, $pass)
    {
        /* No change here
        */
        }
    functionget_logged_in_user (  )
    {
        // Will check if there's a login user session and if so will
        // fetch its record
```

```
$ci = &get_instance();

//get the login in user ID, if any
$uid = $this->session->userdata('user_id');
if (! $uid ) return NULL;
$sql = "SELECT *
FROMusers
WHERE id = '$uid' ";

$q = $ci->db->query($sql);
if ($q->num_rows())
{foreach ($q->result() as $row )
  return $row;
  }
return NULL;
}
Function get_user_rec ( $uid ){
  // Will check if there's a login user session and if so will
  // fetch its record
  $ci = &get_instance();
  // get the login in user ID, if any
  if (! $uid ) return NULL;
  $sql = "SELECT *FROM users WHERE id = '$uid' ";
  $q = $ci->db->query($sql);
  if($q->num_rows())
  {foreach ($q->result() as $row ) return $row;
    }
  return NULL;
  }
Function keep_user_feedback ($feedback) {
  $ci = &get_instance();
  $uid_rec = $this->get_logged_in_user ();
  $uid = $uid_rec ? $uid_rec->id: 0;
  /* id email uid feedback timestamp
  */
  $table = 'user_feedback';
  $data = array ( 'feedback'  =>urldecode ($feedback),
    'uid'=>  $uid);
  $ci->db->insert($table, $data);
  }
  Function  get_user_feedbacks ( $uid ) {
    $ci = &get_instance();
    if (! $uid ) return NULL;
    $feedbacks = array();
```

```
    $table = 'user_feedback';
    $sql = "SELECT * FROM  $tableWHERE  uid = '$uid'
    ORDER BY timestamp DESC";
    $q = $ci->db->query($sql);
    if ( $q->num_rows() ) {
      foreach ($q->result() as $row)
      $feedbacks[] = $row;
      }
    return $feedbacks;
    }
  } // End Users_model
```

The logged_in_view.php view file

The PHP view file is located at application/views/logged_in_view.php.
This file was extended with several more services, as described in the previous
examples. The code and inline explanations are as follows:

```html
<!DOCTYPE html">
<meta http-equiv="Content-type" content="text/html;
  charset=utf-8" />
<html>
<head>
<script src="http://code.jquery.com/jquery-latest.js"
  type='text/javascript'></script>
<scriptsrc="http://code.jquery.com/jquery-1.8.2.js"></script>
<script src="http://code.jquery.com/ui/1.9.0/jquery-ui.js">
</script>
<link rel="stylesheet" type="text/css"
  href="<?=base_url(); ?>/css/my_style.css" media="screen" />
<script type='text/javascript'>
// The AJAX handler controller method URLs
varsave_user_feedback_submitter =
  '<?=site_url()?>'+'index.php/ajax_handler/save_user_feedback';
varget_user_feedbacks = '<?=site_url()?>'
  +'index.php/ajax_handler/get_user_feedback_log';
functionajax_save_user_feedback (feedback) {
  $.ajax({
    type : "POST",
    url : save_user_feedback_submitter,
    data : {feedback: feedback},
    dataType: "json",
    success: function(data) {
      // When AJAX return back alert
      // ('Your feedback Updated - Thanks!');
```

```
        }
      });
    }

  functionajax_get_user_feedback_log() {
    $.ajax({
      type: "POST",
      url: get_user_feedbacks,
      dataType: "json",
      success: function(data) {
        $('#feedback_log_view').show();
        $('#feedback_log_view').html(data.result);
        }
      });
    }
  $(document).ready(function() {
    // Set up the jQuery UI feedback dialog
    $("#ideas-form").dialog({
      autoOpen: false,
      height: 270,
      width: 700,
      modal: true,
      resizable: false,
      effect: 'drop',
      direction: "up",
      show: "slide",
      buttons: {
        "Send Us Your Feedback": function() {
          varuser_feedback = $('#user_feedback').val();
          ajax_save_user_feedback(user_feedback);
          // clean feedback entry for next one
          $('#user_feedback').val('');
          // Show user all its feedback so far
          ajax_get_user_feedback_log();
          $(this).dialog("close");
          },
        "Cancel": function() {
          $(this).dialog("close");
          }
        }
      });

    // When user clicks on for a popup feedback window
    $('#user_ideas').button().click(function() {
```

```
    $("#ideas-form").dialog("open");
    });

   $('#feedback_log').button().click(function() {
   ajax_get_user_feedback_log();
   });
  });// Document ready section
</script >
</head>
<body>
<H1>Welcome <?=$user_name; ?>! </H1>
<H1>You are logged in! </H1>
<HR></HR>
  <H3>Your User ID is: <?=$uid; ?></H3>
  <H3>Your System Role is: <?=$role; ?></H3>
  <H3>Your Menu options: <?=$menu; ?></H3>
<DIV>
  <button id='user_ideas' style="
   cursor: pointer; position: relative; top:0px"
    title='Share your feedback/ideas'>
       Add A New Feedback </button><BR/>
  <button id="feedback_log" style=
    "cursor: pointer; position: relative; top:0px"
       title="Your feedback log"> See Your Feedback Log </button>
</DIV>
  <div id='feedback_log_view' style=
    "display: none; width: 800 px; border-style: solid;
      border-color: black; overflow-x: auto; height: 200 px;
        overflow-y: auto;">
</DIV>
<H2><?php echo anchor
  ('index.php/auth/logout', 'Logout')?></H2>

  <div id= "ideas-form", title= "Your Feedback To Improve">
<form>
<fieldset>
<span id= "user_name" class= "text ui-widget-content
  ui-corner-all"> Thanks <? = $user_name; ?>,
    Please share your feedback with us</span>
<textarea name= "idea_desc", id = "user_feedback", rows = "10"
  cols = "83", placeholder = 'Your ideas'></textarea>
</fieldset>
</form>
</div>
</body>
</html>
```

Summary

In this chapter, we have reviewed the CI views, scope as well as their general MVC scope, and the different types of views and usage. In addition, we showed how to integrate our CodeIgniter code with the third-party template plugin (the CI library, configuration, and additional code assets) for providing the view template services to the application controllers.

We have also learned the examples of integrating the jQuery UI and AJAX in the CI view with the CI controllers/models.

Appendix

In this appendix, we will provide a set of proactive updates and web resources regarding the CodeIgniter community and its featured CI-based sites.

CI formal resources are as follows:

- CI developer Ellis Labs: `http://ellislab.com/codeigniter`
- CI forms for different topics: `http://ellislab.com/forums`
- CI developer online chat: `http://ellislab.com/codeigniter/irc`
- CI user guide: `http://ellislab.com/codeigniter/user-guide`
- CI developments of the community GitHub: `https://github.com/EllisLab/CodeIgniter`
- CI downloads center: `http://ellislab.com/codeigniter/user-guide/installation/downloads.html`

Featured CI plugins are as follows:

- CI sparks — plugin library: `http://getsparks.org/packages/browse/latest`
- CI-based CMS PyroCMS: `https://www.pyrocms.com`
- CI grid plugin: `http://www.grocerycrud.com`
- CI GoCart — e-commerce plugin: `http://gocartdv.com`
- CI PayPal Library: `https://www.x.com/devzone/articles/paypal-library-for-php-codeigniter-framework`
- CodeIgniter Google Maps V3 API Library: `http://biostall.com/codeigniter-google-maps-v3-api-library`
- Facebook PHP SDK and CodeIgniter: `http://www.dannyherran.com/2011/02/facebook-php-sdk-and-codeigniter-for-basic-user-authentication`

- Agile toolkit for CodeIgniter developers: `http://agiletoolkit.org/blog/agile-toolkit-for-codeigniter-developer`
- CI FormIgniter—easy form generator for CodeIgniter: `http://formigniter.org`
- CI Wiki—libraries/plugins for CodeIgniter: `https://github.com/EllisLab/CodeIgniter/wiki/_pages`
- Ajax library wrapper for CodeIgniter: `https://github.com/EllisLab/CodeIgniter/wiki/AJAX-for-CodeIgniter`

Sites and articles supporting CodeIgniter are as follows:

- CI built-in libraries navigator `http://apigen.juzna.cz/doc/EllisLab/CodeIgniter/index.html`
- PHP assist—CodeIgniter project hosting `http://phpassist.com`
- Simply CodeIgniter `http://www.simplycodeigniter.com`
- NetTuts+ CodeIgniter `http://net.tutsplus.com/?s=codeigniter`
- The CodeIgniter tutorials site `http://video.derekallard.com`
- Using CodeIgniter for PHP application development `http://www.macronimous.com/resources/using_codeigniter_for_PHP_application_development.asp`
- CodeIgniter-powered sites—proactively updated list `http://poweredsites.org`
- CodeIgniter site projects `http://seeroo.com/tag/codeigniter`

Featured websites powered by CodeIgniter are as follows:

- Sprint Center `http://www.sprintcenter.com/`
- AT&T Center `http://www.attcenter.com`
- World Gold Council `http://www.gold.org`
- Motortopia `http://www.motortopia.com`
- Club 3D `http://www.club-3d.com`
- Cyber Ears `http://www.cyberears.com`

For more information, refer to the *Build on CodeIgniter* section at `http://ellislab.com/codeigniter`.

Index

Symbols

.htaccess file 9

A

admin user login 55
AJAX 150
Ajax_handler 161
App Garden 76
application/config folder 9
application/controller/auth.php controller 55
application/controllers folder 9
application/helpers folder 10
application/libraries folder 10
application/models folder 9
application/models/users_model.php 55
application/views folder 9
application/views/logged_in_view.php 55
application/views/login_view.php 55
Asynchronous JavaScript and XML. *See* AJAX
attachments
   e-mail, sending with 52
authentication flowchart 86

B

benefits, CI libraries
   simplicity 65
built-in helpers
   using 110
built-in helpers example
   controller file 110
   view file 111

built-in libraries
   using 69
built-in libraries example
   about 69
   controller file 70
   view file 71
business logic 122
business logic example
   about 132
   controller file 132
   model file 133, 139
   view file 136, 140

C

called controller method 143
CGI (Common Gateway Interface) 8
CI
   configurations, defining 29
   configurations, using 29
   miscellaneous naming conventions 39
CI controller
   extending 45, 46
   scope 43
   use cases 46, 48
CI formal resources 169
CI form helper
   about 148
   functions 148
CI forums
   URL 109
CI helpers
   about 107, 109
   accessing 148
   CI system helpers 109
   CI third party helpers 109

T

third-party libraries example
about 71
controller file 72, 75
view file 75

U

user-defined CI controller 44
users_model resource services
get_logged_in_user() 162
keep_user_feedback() 162
UX (User Experience) 154

V

view
about 144
complex parameters, passing to 12
view file linked-company-updates.php 101
view_params 146
view template plugin
rendering 153

W

World Gold Council
URL 170

About Packt Publishing

Packt, pronounced 'packed', published its first book "*Mastering phpMyAdmin for Effective MySQL Management*" in April 2004 and subsequently continued to specialize in publishing highly focused books on specific technologies and solutions.

Our books and publications share the experiences of your fellow IT professionals in adapting and customizing today's systems, applications, and frameworks. Our solution based books give you the knowledge and power to customize the software and technologies you're using to get the job done. Packt books are more specific and less general than the IT books you have seen in the past. Our unique business model allows us to bring you more focused information, giving you more of what you need to know, and less of what you don't.

Packt is a modern, yet unique publishing company, which focuses on producing quality, cutting-edge books for communities of developers, administrators, and newbies alike. For more information, please visit our website: www.packtpub.com.

Writing for Packt

We welcome all inquiries from people who are interested in authoring. Book proposals should be sent to author@packtpub.com. If your book idea is still at an early stage and you would like to discuss it first before writing a formal book proposal, contact us; one of our commissioning editors will get in touch with you.

We're not just looking for published authors; if you have strong technical skills but no writing experience, our experienced editors can help you develop a writing career, or simply get some additional reward for your expertise.

CodeIgniter 1.7 Professional Development

ISBN: 978-1-84951-090-5   Paperback: 300 pages

Become a CodeIgniter expert with professional tools, techniques and extended libraries

1.   Learn expert CodeIgniter techniques and move beyond the realms of the User Guide

2.   Create mini-applications that teach you a technique and allow you to easily build extras on top of them

3.   Create CodeIgniter Libraries to minimize code bloat and allow for easy transitions across multiple projects

CodeIgniter 1.7

ISBN: 978-1-84719-948-5   Paperback: 300 pages

Improve your PHP coding productivity with the free compact open source MVC CodeIgniter framework!

1.   Clear, structured tutorial on working with CodeIgniter for rapid PHP application development

2.   Careful explanation of the basic concepts of CodeIgniter and its MVC architecture

3.   Use CodeIgniter with databases, HTML forms, files, images, sessions, and email

Please check **www.PacktPub.com** for information on our titles

Ext JS 4 Web Application Development Cookbook

ISBN: 978-1-84951-686-0   Paperback: 488 pages

Over 110 easy-to-follow recipes backed up with real-life examples, walking you through the basic Ext JS features to advanced application design using Sencha's Ext JS

1. Learn how to build Rich Internet Applications with the latest version of the Ext JS framework in a cookbook style

2. From creating forms to theming your interface, you will learn the building blocks for developing the perfect web application

3. Easy to follow recipes step through practical and detailed examples which are all fully backed up with code, illustrations, and tips

Responsive Web Design with HTML5 and CSS3

ISBN: 978-1-84969-318-9   Paperback: 324 pages

Learn responsive design using HTML5 and CSS3 to adapt websites to any browser or screen size

1. Everything needed to code websites in HTML5 and CSS3 that are responsive to every device or screen size

2. Learn the main new features of HTML5 and use CSS3's stunning new capabilities including animations, transitions and transformations

3. Real world examples show how to progressively enhance a responsive design while providing fall backs for older browsers

Please check **www.PacktPub.com** for information on our titles